The Old Lonesome

PUBLISHED BY SWEETGRASS BOOKS,
AN IMPRINT OF FARCOUNTRY PRESS, HELENA, MONTANA.

The Old Lonesome

Carol Benson

Sweetgrass Books

AN IMPRINT OF FARCOUNTRY PRESS

For the Deers and the Skunks

We come and go, but the land is always here.

And the people who love it and

understand it are the people

who own it—for a little while.

WILLA CATHER — *"O Pioneers!"*

Sheridan County, Montana

To Regina

Canada

Whitetail

Daleview

Outlook

Old Lonesome

Raymond

16

Dooley

Comertown

Westby

To Fortuna

To Scobey

Plentywood

5

Flaxville

Redstone

Archer

Big Muddy Creek

Antelope

To Grenora →

258

Reserve

Brush Lake

Dagmar

Medicine Lake

Medicine Lake

Sheridan County Line

Fort Peck Indian Reservation

Homestead

North Dakota

Froid

16

To Wolf Point

Poplar

2

Big Muddy Creek

Culbertson

N

Missouri River

To Sidney

The Old Lonesome

Rattlesnakes

ONE OF MY EARLIEST CLEAR MEMORIES is of rattlesnakes. They were not actually seen very often in the furthest northeastern corner of Montana, but we girls could feel their lurking presence. Where we lived, we were used to extremes of weather and fairly peculiar manifestations of the natural world, but one summer in the mid-1950's a veritable plague of rattlesnakes was visited upon us. And along with the unprecedented numbers of serpents came a record-breaking heat wave. During daylight hours, a mirage of wavering thermic rays rose up from the highway running between Redstone and Plentywood. This made the road seem like a river of still-smoldering lava that had cut its way through the limestone acclivities and across the fields of parched grain. Then, as the blacktop cooled down at night, snakes by the hundreds came crawling on to meet their doom, bodies to be smashed under truck tires in the dark and fried into curving strips of leathery bacon in the next day's heat.

Those shriveled snake bodies were strangely, repulsively fascinating to my older sisters and me, riding in Dad's sloped-back black Chevrolet sedan. With noses pressed against the halfway rolled-down windows, we made a game of spotting letters of the alphabet in the flattened snake bodies, or we tried to tally up the total carcasses, though it was impossible to count them all, before we reached the dirt road turnoff to Gramp Walt's farm.

The usually pale yellow prairie grass which covered the rolling hills was desiccated into brittle sticks of brown that summer, and on the Mary Olsen place, an ancient granary and hilltop by the highway, the grayed wood of the building blended sadly into the dried grass color. Mary Olsen had homesteaded her 160 acres early in the first decade of the new century, as had many other women in eastern Montana, and my grandfather, Walter Janson, had purchased her land when she grew too old to manage it herself during the 1930's. Despite transferred ownership to Gramp Walt, that piece of land was thereafter, and for eternity, called the Mary Olsen place. A piece of land was more than a person's property that could simply be transferred by deed in hardscrabble Sheridan County; a piece of land represented a lifetime of struggle against heavy odds. Mary Olsen's very soul was bound up in the fragile gray building anchored to the round hilltop, and her everlasting spirit was abloom in the modest showing of wild sunflowers that persisted next to her granary.

"Hi, Mary," we girls chorused out the windows as Dad gunned the car up the rock encrusted dirt road circling her hill. My sisters and I had often wondered about the personal qualities of Miss Mary Olsen, whose name had been known to us for as long as we could remember, and we had imagined at length the possibilities for her physical appearance and character. We had at last settled on a probable picture of Mary as a red-cheeked and large-boned woman like our Scandinavian grandmother, a woman who was spirited, determined, and sturdy enough to homestead her own place like a man. We decided that she had worn her light brown hair braided and coiled into a massive crown atop her head, and she had worn for her everyday clothes a long, full gingham dress with checks of sky blue to enhance her pale eyes, and over that simple frock, a stiff canvas apron would rebuff the homestead dust and soil. We pictured her wearing big brown boots and a wide straw hat as she tromped through the fields that were hers. Before I started school and learned about the subtleties of spelling, I believed that her name described a personal sunniness of disposition: that Mary was merry.

Beyond her place, the road soon narrowed into two dirt tire tracks winding over the hills, and as we passed along, the tall grasses in the center section slapped at the bottom of our Chevy. Often we heard meadowlarks trilling in the fields on the way to the farm. My sisters and I looked eagerly for them, but their yellow and gray feathers blended so well with the dry prairie that our serenaders remained unseen. But the magpies were not so modest; harsh squawks arose as the sound of our car startled them off their fence post perches and into flight, their black-and-white bodies stark against the brilliant blue sky. And higher up in that vast space of sky we might catch sight of a hawk, dark and strong, in an endless and leisurely glide.

We three girls knew all the neighboring spreads. Frode Larsen's place was next to our grandfather's on the east, Judd Anderson's place verged on the west, and High Pockets Peterson's land was just over the next hill. "Neighboring" was a relative term, though, with vast fields of hard wheat, oats, barley, and sometimes flax, separating the homestead centers. Frode's farm buildings stood, some just barely due to age and wind, right next to the dirt road passage and his old-fashioned wooden windmill pumped ferociously when the northeastern wind blew. As we followed the dirt road, we marked the progress of each farmer's fields, comparing them to those of our grandfather. None of the farmers lived on his farm anymore. All of them had long since moved into our bustling town of Plentywood, the county seat and a community of two thousand, with businesses, homes, and churches clustered together closely, as if standing in determined solidarity against the very vastness of the landscape.

"Hooray, I saw it first!" yelled out Lavinia, the eldest of us, as she spotted the Shade Tree, a lone oak standing in the open space it had chosen as residence perhaps a hundred years before. The surrounding land was bare prairie at the time when the oak planted itself, but now it stood right in the middle of Frode's wheat field. It would have made his plowing and combining much simpler if Frode had just chopped the tree down and dragged out its stump with his tractor, but that he would never do. An oak was a rarity there and the size of this one remarkable, and it had come to serve as an unspoken symbol of stability and tenacity to the farmers who passed by it. It was a landmark in those treeless parts and its shade provided a lunchtime oasis to Frode and his hired crew. To us it indicated that Gramp's farm was around the next bend in the road.

Dad turned off the rocky dirt road and onto a softer dusty one through a field of summer fallow, past a windbreak of silvery Russian olive trees, and into the big open yard of Old Lonesome, our grandfather's homestead. Grandpa Walt owned about a thousand acres of farmland fanning into the Great Plains periphery to the north and to the west of Plentywood, but the headquarters of his farm was the forty-year-old unpainted shack in the center of his original homestead. He had chosen to call his place Old Lonesome in those early days when it occupied the prairie without any neighboring farms, only the incessant wind to keep it company.

Walter had tried many jobs as a young man growing up in a land that was far from lush. At the age of twelve he left home to become the chore-boy on a cattle ranch near Comertown, and after a couple of years he was promoted to cowboy. His days of riding herd were long and hard, but full of adventure for a young man on the wide open plains. Those days had ended when fences began to spring up and cordon off the land, controlling the vast range and demarcating it into spreads of private ownership. In need of work, Walter had gotten a more stationary position raising sheep on the Lundquist ranch outside of Scobey. Then he took the job of manager for the lone store and post office at Flaxville, a settlement consisting of three houses, which proved to be an unbearably isolated outpost for the quiet but gregarious Scandinavian bachelor. When he'd had his fill of solitude, he moved to the booming town of Redstone, where he operated a gasoline station for the automobiles that were beginning to replace horse and buggy rigs.

At last, having tried the various possibilities open to a strong young Swede with a fourth grade education, Walter married our grandmother, a Norwegian woman who was nine years his senior, and one of the area's few schoolteachers. Now he settled down to the life of a farmer. They combined her homestead land with his to create a good-sized spread. The government required that a house be built on a claim that was to be proved up, a proviso that was truly a challenge in that unforested land, but with the help of his two brothers, Walter foraged and salvaged enough pieces of wood to construct a honeymoon nest of sorts for his bride. Thereafter Walter used to say, "If a Swede and a Norwegian can live together in a twelve foot shack, well sure then, I guess anybody can get along." By the 1950's his shack had withstood decades of powerful prairie winds, dust storms, howling blizzards, and tempests of oversized hailstones, but despite its triumph over all of these assaults, it stood with the humble demeanor of its owner.

As we girls leaped out of the car, Gramp waved to us from across the yard, "Hi Vinny, hi Alex, hi there Junior!" He was working the hand pump to fill buckets of precious water from his deep-drilled well. Most summers he kept that water in reserve below the ground because the big wooden barrel by the shack usually collected enough melted snow and spring rainfall to keep his vegetable garden watered. The barrel also collected a whole array of insects in the rain water, floundering grasshoppers waiting to be saved by an offered blade of grass, and already-drowned bugs of many sizes and glittering colors floating like little pieces of a crazy kaleidoscope on the water's surface. That summer, however, the barrel was bone dry.

We ran to the pump eagerly.

"Can we help you, Gramp?"

"Yeah, sure, girls. The vegetables need some weeding and watering. Junior's too little to haul the buckets so she'll be a weeder. Alex, you go with her and Vinny can haul the water."

"Look out for snakes," our grandfather added. Gramp used to repeat an old saying about how rattlesnakes seldom traveled north of the town of Culbertson because they didn't like to swim all the way across the Missouri River, but this summer he had been silent about their geographic range. He was one of the few men in the county who disliked hunting and would not choose to harm even a snake. He hoped the rampant rattlesnakes would respect his peaceful nature and stay off his property.

The vegetable patch was a long dusty rectangle edging one side of the farmyard. Through the cracked light-gray soil struggled rows and rows of corn, peas, beans, tomatoes, beets, and carrots, and a whole end of the garden was given over to mounds of potato plants. Alex and I started tugging at the weeds invading the corn rows, skinny-stemmed stinkweeds, named for a cabbage-like odor emanating from their tiny white blossoms, and large, dark, stickery weeds easy to spot next to the smooth emerald-colored corn stalks. Weeds never seemed to be bothered much by the heat and drought conditions—in the face of adversity they would thrive.

"I wonder if we'll get good corn this year. It wasn't knee-high by the fourth of July like it should have been," mused Alex, "and now it's barely past my shoulders."

"I'm already hungry," I replied. I skipped down the path between the rows to the other end of the garden, raising puffs of powdery dust that coated the plants in my wake. Eagerly I dug with my fingers into the hard dirt surrounding a big carrot, then grasping it by the neck, I eased it out of the grip of the earth. I rubbed most of the dirt off onto my jeans, then crunched into the warm sweetness of the orange flesh. Even with the challenge of eating without my top front teeth, nothing in the world tasted better than a carrot just yanked from the ground. I scraped off the last bits of orange with my bottom teeth and tossed the feathery stalk into the dry grass beyond the garden patch, then I knelt down to pick another.

"You'd better get back to work, Jeanne!" Alex called out. "We're both supposed to be pulling weeds." When she tried to boss me, Alex used my given name.

"Don't be so bossy, Alexandra, I'm working for Gramp, not you!" I snapped back. I returned to the spot where I had stopped weeding. We two worked along in silence, moving slowly in parallel rows and feeling the sun getting hotter on our backs through our thin cotton shirts. I could still taste sugary bits of the carrot stuck in my teeth. I was working my hardest to pull out my weeds faster than Alex and beat her to the end of the row.

But then, both of us stopped abruptly as we heard a slow, gentle rattling sound. Silently we rose from crouching and stared at the other, each standing as death-still as the prairie when the wind stops blowing. Out of all that stillness I could hear the blood thumping in my ears, steady and hard. The resonant pound of my blood muffled the sound of the rattling while the sun glared down on my head, and then all noises ceased. I felt the whole world to be utterly soundless. But no, with a startling proximity, the rattling came again, insistent, louder, faster. Time did not move and neither could we in that hot corn patch. I looked desperately at Alex. She was the big sister so she should do something to save us, I thought, but her face was blank, her mouth slightly open.

As the terrible sound loudened again, I repeated in my mind all that I had heard about rattlesnakes: how they were supposed to be shy and would not bother you if you didn't move at all, but how if they had already coiled up they would strike out and bite you, and how if they did bite you, you must get someone to tie a tight handkerchief around your arm or leg to block your blood from circulating and then the person must cut you with a knife and suck out all the poison so you would not die, and they had to do all this within a half hour or you would die anyway. I tried to stay perfectly still but now I could feel my knees shaking under my jeans and they shook harder and harder until I thought I would fall over into the dirt and the rattler would just bite me on the face and probably no one, not even Gramp, would be able to suck the poison out then.

Suddenly something leaped out from behind the corn row and knocked me hard to the ground. I thrashed desperately in the dirt as I tried to crawl away from the horrible killer snake, but then I heard the helpless laughter of Vinny, soon joined by hesitant giggles from Alex. Looking up I saw the handful of little wooden cones Vinny was shaking in my face, colored gamepieces from the SORRY board game kept in the shack. "Oh, I'm so SORRY!" Vinny gasped as she laughed at me lying there in the dirt. I turned my face away so Vinny couldn't see the tears streaming into streaks of mud on my filthy cheeks. Then, still chortling, Vinny picked up her empty buckets and trudged back to the pump.

We continued the weeding and watering until the rows were finished. The wet mud around the plants made an almost startling stain of rich umber against the gray soil, color that faded quickly in the intense heat. Then we went to wash our hands and faces at the pump, where Vinny worked the big handle up and down, up and down, until at last the water flowed in a gush out of the curving metal spout. We crossed the yard to the shack to find shade from the hot sun.

We could hear Gramp's soft voice through the screen door, a rickety affair lightly held together with lathing and patches but serving as an effective barrier against the horseflies.

"Bud, you know you shouldn't bring your Drink out here. Your mother cannot abide it."

We stopped in our tracks, surprised to hear Gramp make a criticism. He did so extremely rarely and it did not fit his way of talking, but we knew that Grandma Christina strongly opposed any kind of Drink. She called it "The Devil's Poison," and she said it had destroyed as many people in the world as war and famine. Drink could lead the righteous into evil and sinning and then the everlasting punishment of Hell's fires.

Hearing Gramp's gently chiding words, we stayed outside and just waited for a moment. We liked hearing our father called Bud rather than Oscar. Bud had been his nickname when he starred on the Plentywood High School basketball team, the Wildcats. Our father was a tall and handsome man with dimples that appeared when he smiled, deep as the ocean blue eyes, and thick, wavy black hair, surprising hair for a half-Swedish and half-Norwegian man. Now he talked back rudely to his father, "Damn it, I'm a grown man." But he put the beer can back into a paper bag.

Gramp saw us there on the step. "Come in, girls, cool down, and have some bloat." Bloat was known as Pepsi-Cola to most of the world, but Gramp had coined his own term to aptly describe the feeling of drinking a whole bottle. There was no ice ever to be had in that shack fed with only sporadic electricity, and the sweetness of the bloat was intensified by its warmth, but it quenched nonetheless. Vinny sat down on the unpainted wooden chair vacated by our father, and Alex and I crowded together onto the other one. The rough floor of the shack was covered with unmatched strips of scrap linoleum, and one long piece with aqua water patterns seemed to temper the dry heat seeping in from outside.

"Did my helpers finish up in the garden?" Gramp asked as he poured our drinks into old jelly jar glasses.

"Yes we did!" Vinny answered, glancing over at me, one eyebrow slightly raised, checking to see if I planned to report the rattlesnake scare. But I had learned through many trials that it was best not to tattle on my oldest sister so I averted my eyes with spurious dignity and just sipped at my warm bubbly bloat. Next to me on the chair, Alex smiled in amusement.

Having two lively sisters a few years older inspired me to start walking at a very early age, I had been told. My smaller body's persistence in tagging after Vinny and Alex, trying to keep up with their activities and play in their games, had finally earned me their grudging respect and status as a junior member of their sister club, thus the moniker Junior. I was constantly being reminded that junior meant lower in rank as well as age.

Finished with the chores, revived by the drink, we headed back outside to play. Sometimes we brought along our softball and bat from home and practiced throwing and batting in the open space of the farmyard. This had not been possible the previous summer when Gramp had experimented with raising turkeys. The big giddy creatures were given the run of the farmyard and they chased and attacked us, particularly me because I was barely taller than they were. I was terrified to have the berserk birds charging after me, and when they caught up, they pecked and bloodied my toes through my sandals. Gramp told us that although turkeys were big bullies they were not very smart. If rain began to fall they would hold their beaks open and tilted skyward to try to drink, and if the rain turned into a downpour they would stand there drinking until they drowned. I kept hoping for lots of rain so that I could see those horrid turkeys drown, but that summer was as dry as usual. After just one season Gramp decided the turkeys were too temperamental and so he went back to raising chickens, relatively docile creatures content to sit and lay eggs in the henhouse or step carefully around their fenced-in yard. Vinny always liked to give them a little excitement, though, and she would climb up onto their house to leap off the roof, startling the more skittish among them and making the reddish brown feathers fly. These feathers we carefully collected to use in playing Indians.

I was rather abruptly introduced to the other use of the hens one Saturday when Dad decided that fried chicken would be good for Sunday dinner. He pulled a plump victim across the big yard to the shack and pushed its neck onto the wooden step. "What are you doing, Daddy?" I cried when I saw the struggling hen, but just then I knew as my father lifted up the axe, and swish, he'd chopped off the chicken's head. I was horrified and stood there speechless. We girls could distinguish between the hens and we had given all of them names. I was trying to figure out if my father had just murdered Red Polly or Penny, and then the utterly unimaginable happened. The headless chicken got up and took off running in a big arc around the farmyard, its bloody neck rising above its fat body and flicking drips of gore into a trail behind it as it ran. With an irresistible interest my eyes followed the ghastly being as it circled and circled until finally it dropped to the ground.

"I guess no one told her she was dead," Dad laughed.

OUR FAVORITE DESTINATION for play was the Coulee, a low area dropping down from one side of the homestead yard, so named by our grandfather, I thought then, because it stayed much cooler there in hot weather. Gramp's Coulee was a gentle valley where melting snow would collect in the spring and form a lovely small lake that usually lasted halfway through the summer before drying up. A little forest of cottonwoods insisted on surviving there in the protection of the slopes, with a jungle of chokecherry trees bordering on one edge.

Wild roses bloomed a soft pink near the lake bed, and their discreet fragrance was drawn out by the sun's warmth. In the early summer clusters of bluebells covered the slopes of the Coulee. They had delicately arching stems covered with flowers of a periwinkle blue like the winter sky between snowstorms, and the inside of each bell was shaded purple. Later the untamed alfalfa bloomed in many tints of lavender, and native clover produced tiny yellow blossoms from which we liked sucking out the nectar like bees. Clumps of wild sunflowers with rich golden petals grew tall and we could pluck their tough stems to make bouquets.

But the most magical flower of all had no name and was not even very pretty. It came from a bluish-gray plant that grew very low to the ground and produced a few skinny stems, each with a small cone-shaped spike of dark-lavender flowers, some spikes bald on top like Friar Tuck. These precious tiny flowers produced the most lovely scent possible, an aroma like ripe strawberries mixed with lilacs. Our father could identify every plant in the area, so we asked him once what this special flower was called. Surprisingly, he did not know a name for it.

The little flowers were an elusive treasure of that harsh landscape and sometimes did not appear for years at a time. They surely must have hidden themselves during that burning summer when the legions of rattlesnakes came, but of this we were not certain. The three of us were forbidden to go into the Coulee because Gramp thought that the snakes might seek out its cooler recesses too.

"LET'S PLAY STAGECOACH," suggested Alex.

"I want to be the driver this time, okay?" I begged.

"No, you're too little and scared of things. The driver must be tough and brave. I will drive and Alex can ride shotgun and you will be the passenger," Vinny decided. I was the perpetual passenger.

We raced across the yard to Gramp's oldest piece of farm equipment, a metal and wood plowing contraption that had been pulled by a team of horses to break up the clumps of hard soil in the early days of the homestead. It had a long wooden tongue, and to this Vinny hitched her invisible horses. She and Alex squeezed into the molded metal driver's seat, and I climbed up behind them onto the frame of the plow. Alex clutched a stick for her shotgun, and Vinny clicked, "Gee, Haw, Boys!" as she shook the imaginary reins. We were off.

All of Gramp's ancient tractors and other obsolete machines were spread around the circumference of the big yard along with the plow and disk harrow that were still used. The old pieces of equipment were faded in color from years of standing motionless in bright sun and harsh weather, but they were preserved without rust in that dry land.

His newest and largest pieces of machinery were kept protected in a metal quonset, a long arched building that resembled an airy cave inside. With the big sliding doors pulled shut, a trio of noisy girls could make our shouts and singing echo deeply through the space. The machines were parked very tightly next to each other by Gramp's skillful maneuvering and their vivid colors were cheerful in the dull galvanized interior of the quonset. His new tractor was a bright green color, the giant grain-hauling truck had a blue cab and red slatted body, and the Minneapolis Moline (a name I considered immensely satisfying to pronounce) combine was golden orange. Gramp's grain auger looked like a silvery giraffe without a body, just a long, long neck with a tapered head, precariously mounted on small wheels. It stood upright by the sliding door as if posted to guard the other pieces of equipment, and I always felt we should slip past it quickly when sneaking into the quonset to climb on Gramp's huge machines or play hide-and-seek around them. Once inside, we had to step as carefully as chickens over the puddles of gritty oil on the concrete floor.

The older pieces of equipment offered more possibilities for play because they were loose in the outdoors and we could imagine them traveling miles and miles beyond the confines of the quonset structure. Then, too, many of them had built-in metal toolboxes containing odd-shaped tools and we were allowed to tinker as much as we pleased on the outdated machines. Bluish tin caps the size of a quarter covered vital parts of the machinery that needed oil, and we made a game of finding them on the undersides and in the crannies of the machines, then prying them open to add imaginary oil, as we imagined Gramp doing many years before. We liked to think of the olden days on the farm when Dad was the boy called Bud who helped his father in the fields, spending long hours plowing and planting, then working in harvest alongside the hired crew.

But now, "Time to go, kiddos," Dad yelled, "alllllllllll aboard!"

Vinny made the imaginary stagecoach stop abruptly and we jumped off it to switch to more up-to-date transportation.

"Gramp, can I ride with you?" I hopped up onto the running board of his turquoise Chevrolet pickup.

"Okay, little one," he answered.

"Me too?" asked Vinny.

"Sure, Vinny."

Alex climbed into the front seat of Dad's car, the place where Vinny usually sat, and the black sedan headed out of the farmyard. Vinny and I joined Gramp in the pickup, me in the middle, and I sat on my knees to watch Dad's Chevy pass through the summer fallow, kicking up a cloud of dirt as it went. The loose dust floated sideways and settled on the trees of the windbreak, a light coating indistinguishable from the dun-colored bark and the grayish-green leaves of the oleasters.

"Wow, Dad's really going fast," Vinny remarked, to which Gramp quietly answered, "Yup." Gramp followed slowly to let Dad's dust settle.

The pickup passed by a field pierced with a gully into which Walter and his son had heaved hundreds of granite boulders over the years. The speckled rock surfaces made a tweed-like pattern inside the ravine, with patchwork variations of color among the stones and the bushy weeds. The wide countryside was studded with such boulders, and every year as the fields were plowed giant new stones appeared as if they had propelled themselves upward with a pernicious force from the bowels of the earth just to try the patience of the good farmers of Sheridan County. Many farmers made use of the middling-sized stones to brace their barbed-wire fence posts against the wind's continuing onslaught. The bigger ones were rolled to lower ground where their accumulation gave evidence of how long an area had been farmed. The little gully by Old Lonesome was pretty well filled up.

Gramp sang as we drove along the dirt road toward the highway:

You are my sunshine, my only sunshine
You make me happy when skies are gray
You'll never know, dear, how much I love you
Please don't take my sunshine away

He grinned as he sang the words and his deeply tanned cheeks crinkled up to show creases radiating from the corners of his eyes. When Gramp smiled no one watching him could not smile too. Sitting beside him I felt very small. Across the big seat of the pickup my legs stretched toward the knob of the gear shift and I had to be careful not to kick it. From my place between Vinny and Gramp I could see only the blue sky straight ahead over the turquoise hood of the truck, not the bumpy road through the fields. I scooted close to Gramp and sniffed the familiar smell of oiled machinery mixed with farm soil, the good smell that clung to Gramp when he worked, and always pervaded the cab of his pickup.

The other night, dear, as I lay sleeping,
I dreamt I held you in my arms
When I awoke, dear, I was mistaken
So I hung my head and I cried …

I had to giggle at those last words sung by Gramp. It was absolutely inconceivable that my grandfather would hang his head and cry, and I had never known him to be mistaken about anything. I thought Gramp was one of the smartest men in the world because he knew so much about weather and growing things, and also he could figure out how to fix any problem. When his combine or another piece of machinery broke down he took out his tools and repaired it. He could spot the shape of a cloud and tell you what kind of storm was coming and how soon. And the time he and Dad had discovered ugly gray ticks in all three of our scalps after we girls had spent an afternoon under the trees in the Coulee, Gramp knew the best thing to do. Dad had gotten out his matches and was ready to burn out the ticks, but Gramp said they should use a different method of removing them without fire. He did not want to risk burning the least bit of our hair. Gramp said that the ticks screw themselves clockwise into a person's skin, so they just need to be held onto firmly and unscrewed in the other direction, counterclockwise, and this he had patiently done.

Now the road dropped low and crossed a deep gully where a graceful deer had once been spotted very close-up on one side of the road, and where a skittering skunk had been seen another time on the other side of the passage. Thereafter, whenever our family traveled through the gully, passengers seated on the Deer side of the car were called Deers for the duration of the ride, and those on the other side of the car were teased for being as smelly as Skunks. Whenever Vinny was seated on the Skunk side of the car, she would remember to quickly slide into the middle of the seat, pushing against whoever might be in her way, to avoid being called stinky, but Alex and I usually didn't think of that trick so quickly and then she would taunt us without mercy. On this crossing Gramp was seated on the

Skunk side of the pickup, but no one would ever think of calling him one, so Vinny just smiled smugly and whispered in my ear, "I'm a Deer, but you are half-Skunk!"

As we reached the blacktop leading back to town, Vinny had a sudden idea. Her inspirations were frequent and often troublesome for others in some way, but this one was purely of an empirical nature. "Gramp, can we collect some of the snake bodies? I could use them for the science fair in a couple of months."

Before this summer's epidemic the only rattlesnake actually seen by my sisters and me had been more like the mere ghost of one, the transparent skin shed by a large rattler and left draped across a sandstone trail in the badlands near Glendive. The imprinted patterns of the scales had been lightly visible on the delicate fabric of the skin, and at the tapered end little gauzy pouches remained in the shape of the rattles they had enveloped. This ephemeral incarnation of a fearsome killer was a wonderment to us and we had carefully carried that snakeskin home from our outing. Back at our house the fragile treasure did not last long in its cardboard box display case—it soon crumbled into small flakes of parchment.

"The science fair? Well sure, why not?" Gramp chuckled to himself, then reached for a dusty burlap bag underneath the seat of the truck and handed it to Vinny.

"I want some too," I announced.

As our grandfather watched for any unflattened snakes beside the way, Vinny and I walked along the gravelly shoulder of the road and onto the highway, and she collected several of the stiff carcasses. I finally dared to pick one up too. I gripped it in the middle of the snake's body and warily held it at arm's length despite its obvious state of mummification. When Vinny had nearly filled the gunny sack we climbed back into the pickup. Gramp drove back to town, greeting the vehicles we passed on the highway with a farmer's wave, made by raising the first two fingers of his right hand slightly off the steering wheel. If a driver failed to return Gramp's greeting, Vinny looked quickly behind at the passing license plate to see where the stranger came from, most often North Dakota or Saskatchewan.

After school had started and the science fair preparations were underway, Vinny retrieved the bag of dried rattlers from Gramp's garage and the three of us selected what we needed. Vinny decided to do an anatomical analysis of rattlesnakes for her project, showing the parts of the mouth and how they bite, the venom sacs, and the bone structure of the reptile. She used the two straightest of the flattened snakes and mounted them on a piece of plywood, one skin showing the top side of the snake and the other the underside, and she glued on examples of uncrushed bones. Then she drew diagrams of the inside structures of the rattlesnake from various angles, using information from the *World Book Encyclopedia,* and she wrote paragraphs of description to accompany her illustrations.

Alex was interested in the aesthetic aspects of the snakes' bodies. She took the most distinctly colored of the desiccated skins to show the spotted patterning of the Great Plains Rattlesnake. She attached the skin to a sheet of posterboard, and painted a grid of the mosaic-like designs with her watercolors, showing the shape and color variations of the scales and the large ovoid patterns along the snake's back.

Rarely did younger students participate in the science fair but I had my own brilliant idea to develop. I had helped collect the dried snake bodies, one of them anyway, so I was entitled to use the leftover ones. Behind the Red Owl Grocery I found a large piece of cardboard to use for my poster and I dragged it home and into the basement where I could work on it in solitude. I spread out the cardboard in a corner partially hidden by the bulky form of the freezer, and there on the cold floor I worked on my top secret project. The only person I needed to have help me was my mother. I kept asking her to buy more bottles of thick white glue as I used it up. My work consumed several bottles of the stuff.

When my poster was finally finished I was immensely proud of what I had done and I invited my sisters into the basement to take a look. They came down the stairs and over to the corner where I'd been working, skeptical smiles on their faces. I had propped up a flashlight to shine dramatically on my masterpiece of a poster, which was leaning against the wall. "Well, what do you think?" I demanded eagerly.

Vinny and Alex looked at the decorated piece of cardboard for a long moment, their eyes met, and they burst out laughing. Puzzled, I studied my work, trying hard to figure out what they had found so hilarious. The top of my poster was made of carefully arranged snake bodies held in place by great quantities of glue, and on the bottom of the cardboard I had carefully written out my scientific findings in black crayon. The poster said:

SIENCE

You can spell things with snakes.

PLENTY OF WOOD

There was a story that Gramp liked to tell about how our small town got its name.

In the late nineteenth century groups of Scandinavians began to desert the crowded farmlands of Minnesota and move west in search of the unlimited space elicited by the name Great Plains. Many families loaded up the farm wagons with all of their worldly goods that would fit, and boldly set out in search of fertile new fields to cultivate. Some crossed straight through North Dakota and continued on into the grassland of northeastern Montana. Such a group, it may have been Norwegians and it may have been Swedes, was in need of a sheltering place to bed down at the end of their long day and some fuel for their supper campfire. Across the undulating prairie one sharp-eyed fellow spotted a stand of box elder trees and cottonwoods.

"Look!" he called out, "Look! Plenty of wood!" so the weary travelers crossed the gentle hills to make camp under those trees, beside the slow-moving creek which nourished them.

Beneath the everlasting blue sky that brought the morning, and with the benefit of a season of extra-heavy rainfall, the surroundings looked like a Lutheran Garden of Eden to the travelers and they decided to go no further. The name of their settlement was fated to be Plentywood, although the "plenty" was very much comparative in the midst of paucity. The town was platted along the banks of the stream they named Box Elder Creek, a modest offshoot of the longer and wider Big Muddy Creek.

Other settlers soon began pouring into the area to take advantage of the Homestead Act, many traveling by railroad to the nearest regional station at Culbertson, forty-five miles to the south of Plentywood. These rail pioneers included my grandfather's family. His parents, Theodore and Ruth, had filed on a homestead, site unseen, while living in Minnesota, and they and their baby son Rasmus traveled by passenger coach westwards to their new home. Their two older sons, teen-aged Emanuel and nine-year-old Walter, had been required to ride the whole distance in the general freight car to watch over their cows, crates of chickens, housewares, and furniture. Arriving at the end of the line in Culbertson, the family members disembarked from their various accommodations and switched to other transport: a horse for Theodore; wagon for Ruth, the baby, the chickens and other possessions; and shanks' mare for the boys. It took the two of them, armed with sticks of willow, four days to herd the family's cows the sixty miles to the new homestead, located north of Plentywood on the Outlook Bench.

Our great-grandparents Theodore and Ruth spent more than thirty years living on their land claim: he tending to the crops planted in the rocky fields, and she tending to the medical needs of both rural people and town residents. There were no physicians in the area at the time so, having studied nursing back in Minnesota, she found herself to be a much-required practitioner. During her many years of unofficial doctoring Ruth traveled countless miles alone by wagon, day or night as needed, and she lost track of the number of babies she helped to birth. In their sunset years Ruth and Theodore gave up the homestead and moved to a more comfortable life in a small house in Plentywood.

Meanwhile, Gramp had grown up and gotten his own homestead farm with Grandma and they had lived at Old Lonesome for a number of years. After their land was proven up, he and Grandma Christina also moved into town. Our grandfather soon became a very popular man among the citizens of Plentywood, partly because of his good will and witty tongue, and partly because he was the spitting image of Will Rogers. Throughout his life strangers reminded him of this constantly. A conversation might go like this:

Friend of Walter's: "Walt, I'd like you to meet my cousin from back east in Minnesota."

Cousin: "Jiminy crickets! Did anyone ever tell you who you look like?"

Walt: "No. Who's that?"

Cousin: "Will Rogers! You look just exactly like Will Rogers!"

Walt: "Well, you don't say! Really?" He'd scratch his chin and look pleased about the stranger's remarkable observation because he was too polite a man to let on that he had heard the comment hundreds of times before. It privately amused him to see how proud people were of themselves for noticing the resemblance but he would never think of spoiling their fun. He enjoyed other people too much for that.

Citizens of Plentywood frequently begged my grandfather to run for Mayor of our town. They said that he would make a perfect Mayor because he was so honest he would cheat himself before he would think of cheating someone else. They promised him that there would be a landslide in his favor, but Walt would have no part of political machinations. His last real interest in participating in politics came in the 1920's when he was involved with the Farmers Nonpartisan Political League, a Socialist organization. In that decade especially, hardscrabble farmers on the northern plains were having a difficult time making a living because of the enormous profits extracted by the middlemen moving their grain to the markets. Farming had always been a haphazard operation in the harsh clime of northeastern Montana due to the extremes of temperature, the vagaries of weather patterns, and the unpredictable ascensions of granite boulders. And added on to these existing obstacles, the greed of grain elevator owners, brokers, and milling companies nearly succeeded in breaking many farmers. They were ripe for the message of the Socialist organizers who swept in from North Dakota, promising government ownership of grain elevators and mills to even out the profits with Mammon and hail insurance to even out the odds with God.

Walter and his friends Frode and Judd were among the area's grain farmers who gathered at the fairgrounds to hear the socialistic message. They had found that hard wheat, also known as durum, was a dependable grain to grow in their area, and they knew they should be able to feed their young families with their labor, yet they struggled constantly to do so. As farmers throughout the dry eastern farmlands of Montana were recruited to the Nonpartisan League during the 1920's, its membership increased by 20,000 people. That number suggests that a good percentage of the northern area's farmers had joined the workers' political organization, but in later years few of them admitted to having been League members. No one denied reading the organization's publication, however. *The Producers News,* official newspaper of the Nonpartisan League, offered the most complete coverage of local news and social events throughout the county, and these listings and items of gossip drew many readers, especially females, to the Socialist journal.

Members of the two traditional political parties in Sheridan County were startled out of their status quo when in an election halfway through the decade of the 1920's members of the Nonpartisan League won all the major county offices including that of Sheriff. The Socialists maintained their hold on the county government for a few years, then many of the League office holders intensified their beliefs and secretly switched their membership to the Communist Party. As the bleak harvest season of 1932 rolled around, the Communists overtly tried to take over the county with a tour de force campaign for the farmers' votes. My grandfather and his fellow farmers were experiencing extremely tough times in those depression years, subsequently called the "Dirty Thirties" because of the unrelenting drought and resulting dustiness in the area. Many voters were seriously considering the strongly pro-farmer Communist Party platform being proclaimed in speeches around the county that autumn.

It seemed almost a certainty that the Stalinists would soon be establishing a satellite colony on American soil, right there in northeastern Montana, but shortly before the election fate stepped in and decreed otherwise. The now-Communist Sheriff had twin teenage daughters, and in late October one of the girls died suddenly of a ruptured appendix. Such was the Sheriff's popularity that most residents of Plentywood, and many other folks from the farms and small towns around, attended the girl's funeral.

The ceremony was held in the school gymnasium to accommodate the crowds of mourners, and when the people had seated themselves in the rows of wooden chairs stretched across the polished floor, some of them began to gasp and whisper excitedly among themselves.

"Oh well, did you ever....?"

"For sure, I have never in all my days....."

"Land sakes!"

The young woman's open casket had been placed below the basket-ball hoop at the far end of the court, and the section by her head was gracefully draped with her Young Pioneer scarf, while the rest of the small coffin was blanketed by a large red flag of the hammer-and-sickle. This image was starkly alien in the space of the familiar gymnasium. When the ceremony commenced and the usual religious dirges and prayers were excluded, the mourners became dumfounded, then outraged.

This heathen funeral so unsettled the overwhelmingly Lutheran community that citizens could talk of nothing else for days after it. Voters realized they could not condone such foreign godlessness even with the promise of more likely economic survival. They formed what was known as the "Unholy Alliance," a uniting of the Democratic and Republican candidates into a single party to oppose the Communist slate.

In November when the votes were tallied up, the Demo/Rep coalition just barely defeated the Communists. The resulting county government was somewhat discombobulated by such an alliance of traditional foes, and this encouraged the Red Party forces to regroup and plot strategy for again seizing control of Sheridan County. Meanwhile, though, the federal election had brought FDR into power and the New Deal into play. The resulting farm subsidies and socially beneficent programs permanently drove the Communists, and the history of their influence, from the northern plains.

GOVERNMENT PROGRAMS DID NOT INCLUDE road building for the town of Plentywood and many streets were still gravel or just dirt through the 1940's and well into the 50's. Most of the town's earliest houses were located in the Old Townsite, the bottom land next to Box Elder Creek where the founding fathers and mothers had camped some sixty years before. Those houses were box-shaped with second stories, unlike the rectangular ranch houses which were constructed on the flat land and outer edges of town in the post-war boom of the early 1950's.

Grandpa Walt and Grandma Christina lived in a white clapboard house just up the road from the Old Townsite and high enough to escape the flash flood of 1953 when sudden torrential rains caused the reservoir above town to burst free. Neighbors who were at home heard a terrifying roar and had to race up into their attics and stay put until Box Elder Creek and the reservoir water receded three days later. Our grandparents' house was not far from the freight train tracks that bisected the town and within sight of the Farmers' Union grain elevators, several massive structures thrusting seven stories upward to make them skyscrapers above the other buildings in town. The monumental elevators were so impressive against the royal blue summer sky that when Gramp viewed them from his yard, he was prone to nod approvingly and remark, "Sure enough, Plentywood is plenty good."

Our grandparents' house was modest in size and unadorned, and Grandma Christina kept it scrupulously clean and tidy. It was likewise with her person: the seams of her tawny stockings were unfailingly vertical in alignment and every iron gray hair on her head was securely cinched into a large bun resting just above the back of her neck. The severity of her coiffure was in surprising contrast to the very tender skin of her face, with its deep creases spread across the soft contours. At those rare times when Grandma Christina expressed affection toward her granddaughters we were always amazed by the unbelievable softness of her cheeks.

Grandma's gray-carpeted living room contained a wine-colored velvet sofa in an old-fashioned style with deep horsehair cushions that sank low under a sitter, even one as lightweight as I was, and enfolded the person in a padded embrace. A couple of dark fabric armchairs, a brass floor lamp, and a massive radio console were crowded into the rest of the room, along with a small round table holding the plain black telephone.

There was no need for a telephone directory on the table because the operator, Agnes, had her listing of those citizens of the town who had telephones in their homes and their assigned calling numbers, two digits and a letter, which derived from the household's street address. During the hours when the operator was on duty, a person simply lifted the receiver, and Agnes said "Number, please?" then the caller told her the number or name of the party desired, and she made the connection. Agnes had held her job since the telephone system first came to Plentywood and she considered her position as Chief of Communications for the community to be vital. She had been discreetly instrumental in fostering serious political debate at the time of the Sheriff's daughter's Communist funeral.

Our grandmother was an old friend of Agnes, and upon occasion Agnes rang her up just to impart a little news she had heard through one of the party lines. Usually, however, Grandma Christina kept her telephone line unused and open for possible emergencies. When my sisters and I were visiting her, Grandma told us that we must never play with the telephone; it was for important matters only, and we may not even touch it. If it should ring while she was occupied elsewhere in the house, we must call her immediately to come to it.

One afternoon, though, when Grandma Christina was outside hanging her washing on the line, Vinny decided to try an experiment. She picked up the receiver and when Agnes asked, "Number, please?" Vinny was silent.

Again, "Number, please?" And no reply.

"Number, please," Agnes now commanded. Vinny said nothing.

"The num-ber, please," the operator enunciated.

Vinny had heard enough and she playfully thrust the telephone receiver into Alex's hands. Alex put her ear to the receiver, and heard Agnes's controlled, but obviously very annoyed voice: "NUMBER, please." Alex pulled the receiver from her ear, looked at it for a moment, then handed it to me. Puzzled about who was talking, I held the receiver up to my ear.

"NUM-BER, PLEASE!" an angry voice demanded.

"I-I-I-don't know," I whispered.

"You don't know! Why don't you know? Are you PLAYING WITH THE TELEPHONE?" Agnes accused.

"I don't know," I managed to mumble again before Vinny seized the receiver and slammed it down.

We three went into the yard to play Red Light, Green Light, but we knew that we were in trouble when the telephone soon began to ring and ring. Grandma Christina hurried into the house to answer it, and then moments later she reappeared in the yard, those very soft cheeks of hers flaming with anger.

"Agnes told me you were playing with the telephone," she said. "You shan't play with the telephone in my house. You shan't! And if you do, I will whale the living tar out of you! Do you understand me?"

I stared at my grandmother. Grandma Christina was a resourceful and able-bodied woman, and I could clearly imagine her somehow finding a huge whale there, thousands of miles from an ocean, picking it up with her large hands, and swinging its heavy body by the tail, straight at me. I could almost see the whale and feel my living tar draining away....

"Do you understand me?" our grandmother asked the three of us again. We nodded our heads. I would never dare to play with the telephone again.

Christina's progenitors had come from the far north of Norway, a cold and harsh place. From stern, hard-working Lutherans our grandmother had inherited an austere outlook on temporal existence and the useless pursuit of luxuries and frivolities in this life. One April, however, after a violent hailstorm had broken her living room window, she had gone against her natural tendency to have the regular-size window replaced, and instead she had commissioned a large picture window to be installed in the living room. Subsequently, while she dusted her telephone table and her whatnot shelf, Christina could look through this wide opening to see the honeysuckle and lilac bushes which lined her small lawn, and beyond it the unpaved street heading south from town.

The May blooming of lilac bushes announced that spring had arrived at last in our part of the world. The lavender color of the blossoms brightened a plain yard, and their sweet fragrance was intoxicating when wafted about by light winds. Sniffing their heady scent through an open window, Grandma Christina sometimes could not stop herself from bursting into a chorus of *Springtime in the Rockies* in her high, thin voice.

When it's springtime in the Rockies
I'll be coming back to you-ou-ou

Little sweetheart of the mountains,
With your bonny eyes so blue-ue-ue …

Of course she then felt the need to follow such spontaneous excess with a more restrained chorus of a good Lutheran hymn such as *O Lamb of God, I Come, I Come.* In her honeysuckle bushes, long rectangular box elder bugs, dull black with red stripes and a red **X** across their backs, congregated as soon as the pink-and-white blossoms opened and emitted the soft fragrance of a watered-down gardenia. The bugs resembled little vehicles on a highway as they crawled in straight lines along the rough-barked stems and branches of the honeysuckle on their way to a feast of nectar inside the flower tunnels. Vinny, Alex, and I often interrupted the quest for honey by capturing the box elder bugs gently between our palms. Then we would set the bugs on our bare arms so we could feel a tickling sensation as the box elders ran frantically over our skin, seeking escape from the monster-girls. Soon the bugs would remember they had hidden wings to open up and spread out and fly away, and that they would do. When the honeysuckle flowers disappeared from the bushes, the box elder bugs did the same and then transparent red berries appeared on the branches, sparkling like clusters of little glass beads.

Grandma Christina always kept hollyhocks along the side of her white house, and the stiff stalks grew tall with the reflected sunlight, producing wide blossoms crinkled like crepe paper in pale tints of pink, vanilla, and yellow, and deeper shades of maroon and cherry red. Bobbing below them were blue bachelor buttons, many colors of Icelandic poppies, and purple larkspur, all prolifically volunteering in a dry garden that she had sown years before.

Shiny black crickets lived under Grandma Christina's crumbling cement front step, and their melodious chirping filled the small yard when the sun went down. Lightning bugs appeared only sporadically from year to year in northeastern Montana, flitting and dancing as tiny fairies when they flashed their purplish-green glowing lights. The fireflies did not visit the wide open tracts by the newer houses in the community; they preferred to gather in the older sections of town where more closely grouped houses slowed the prairie winds. The hedged-in yard of our grandparents' house attracted a good share of the fireflies, and when Vinny, Alex, and I were visiting there, we cavorted around the grass in dizzy circles in pursuit of the little creatures. One evening Vinny caught a lightning bug in a glass jar and held it up high, saying she'd created a light bulb to brighten the yard, and she kept the tiny prisoner for a long while until Alex finally persuaded her to free it.

A large house stood on the lot across the street from our grandparents' house. It was owned by an elderly man rumored to be cantankerous, but since he was rarely visible on the premises, we sometimes dared to sneak into his unkempt yard to climb the big oak tree there. One time we ventured further into his property, through a jungle of purple-flowered money plants surrounding his propane tank, and there we encountered the largest spiders in the world. We counted seven of them, each securely settled in its own silvery web anchored between the tall weeds and the propane tank, and each with a tremendously fat gray body and ridiculously skinny black legs. Alex and I stared at them from a safe distance, but Vinny crept close enough to scientifically poke at one with a stick. Then, when it lunged suddenly down toward her leg, Alex and I shrieked and tore off running, thrashing our way through the money plants. Vinny followed us, walking calmly. When we reached Grandma's yard, she reported that she had made a scientific identification. The creatures were called Pillow Spiders, she said, and their overstuffed bodies were full of a type of poison more deadly than a rattlesnake's. We were lucky to have escaped their venom.

Except for that one large dwelling, the houses in the old neighborhood were plain and without pretense; their purpose was to protect the inhabitants from the elements and that is what they did. Alex had once traveled with a friend's family to Great Falls and there her artistic eye noticed the gracious Victorian houses, each painted with several lovely colors and decorated with gingerbread detailing. Some had round towers like castles and many had elegant balustrades around their large porches. Later she asked our grandmother why none of the houses in Plentywood had fancy trim, pretty colors, or even outdoor porches.

Grandma Christina thought for a moment. "Land sakes, the people here don't have time for such nonsense. There's not enough time in the day to waste it sitting around on a porch." And she clicked her tongue at the very thought of slothful porch-sitting.

THE MAIN SECTION of Plentywood was laid out squarely in a grid, seven blocks long from north to south, and nine blocks wide from west to east. The center of the grid became the intersection of Main Street and First Avenue, also known as Highway 16, and this busy crossing was efficiently regulated by two stop signs. In the northwestern and southeastern boundaries of the grid a few more streets developed which defied the careful city plan and connected up at acute or obtuse angles, and on these streets sprouted the recently built dwellings of newcomers and the younger families of the community.

One of the modern ranch houses stood by the open fields of prairie verging on the west side of town and facing the flowing hills to the north. This was our family's home, designed by my mother, and painted the unusual color of charcoal gray. Mother drew the floor plan for the building and determined all the detailings of the décor, including the materials, patterns, and colors for the walls and floors of the house. She had designed the windows of the living room to be floor to ceiling, for gazing out at the spacious landscape, but the windows in the bedrooms she had ordered to be small and too highly placed to be looked through, so they served to shut out all views except for a small wedge of that endless Montana sky. Townspeople were a bit perplexed by those very high, horizontally slit windows so reminiscent of the apertures in the city jail, but they knew that Lorraine Janson was not only from out of state, she had also studied art in college. Perhaps those small slits of windows were the latest artistic design, they figured.

The furnishings, too, had been carefully selected by Mother to reflect the most modern ideas in decorating, and many of the town's younger housewives had observed and copied elements of her style.

In the living room, the matching divans were armless, and covered in a light gray, black, and red tweed. They were flanked by two blond wood end tables, one of which held a red telephone, and the other a large glass ashtray. The lamps were simple white cylinders mounted on skinny iron legs. The drapes had been custom-made in material shipped from St. Paul, Minnesota, a Modern Art-inspired fabric with a gray background sectioned with black lines and white, red, and black dominoes. The wall-high fireplace was built of thin yellow-ocher bricks, and the floor was of a pale polished wood, boldly left uncovered.

Through the wide living room windows, the view took in the rock-strewn hills of the Plentywood Golf Club, a challenging nine-hole course covered with infrequently mowed prairie sod. Beyond the golf course the grassy hills continued rolling onward toward Canada. My sisters and I crossed the dirt road to trespass often on the links, wandering through the tall grass in search of lost tees and balls, making footprints in the soft clay surrounding the numbered holes, and climbing up the chalky limestone formations which cut through some of the steeper hillsides. Occasionally we spotted a pair of golfers, or even a trio, on our vast playfield and then we would run and hide from the intruders.

Although she had been a champion golfer in college, our mother now had no time for such activities. She was constantly busy at home with the toddlers, flaxen-haired Katie and the youngest, and only boy, Walter John, a laughing, dimple-cheeked child we called Johnny. Mother allowed us girls to wander freely around the town and she often gave us the fifteen cents each that would get us into the movie show at the Orpheum, where usually a western was playing and probably one we had seen numerous times.

Or the three of us would pick up our piles of borrowed books and walk to the old stone and brown brick building on the corner of First Avenue and Main Street. The library had once been a bank but now it held riches beyond counting in its stacks. It was a great pleasure to spend an afternoon there reading, wandering through the rows and rows of tall wooden bookshelves, and climbing the stepladders in the reference section. When I first began borrowing books with my own library card, my favorites were those written by Thornton Burgess, a series of lively animal stories enclosed like hidden treasures in the dull brown cardboard library editions. Inside I found the engrossing adventures of Billy Possum, Reddy Fox, Jimmy Skunk, and their fellows, animals who wore clothes, walked upright, and talked smartly, all the while living in harmony with their friends and trying to outwit the enemy animals and humans. Those animals dwelt in the Green Meadows, the Green Forest, and the Purple Mountains, all exotically colorful places, I thought, compared to the prairie land around my town.

My older sisters had thicker books to read: the collections of Mary Poppins stories, the Doctor Doolittle tomes, and biographies of famous people. They waited eagerly for new Hardy Boys mysteries to arrive at the library. Sometimes they had to settle for Nancy Drew mysteries, but her adventures were never as thrilling as those of the Hardy Boys, and Nancy often needed rescuing by her boyfriend Ned. Vinny and Alex thought that Nancy was too much of a girly-girl.

ON THE HIGHEST HILL above the Old Townsite, reached from below by a curving gravel road, the Plentywood Cemetery stretched out in uneven rows of stone markers, the treeless final haven for those hardy farmers and town folk whose struggles had ended. They could wish for no fancier coverlet than the rustling yellow prairie grass above them as they slept there, and from the height of that hill they had a clear vantage for rising up into the cerulean sky at the Final Judgment. My sisters and I liked to visit the granite gravestones of our pioneer forbears and honor them with flowers. In May we brought aromatic lilacs cut from our grandmother's yard; in summer we collected red zinnias, bluebottles, and marigolds from our father's garden when it bloomed; and in between, yellow and purple bouquets could be gathered from the ever-present dandelions and alfalfa weed.

Great-Grandfather Theodore Jansor was buried near the center of the cemetery, and his gravestone of dark gray granite was one of the most impressive markers there. His wife Ruth rested beside him, and her smaller stone was often covered with flowers from unknown donors. Among older members of the community, she was considered to be as sainted a woman as a Lutheran might become. People had not forgotten that she had delivered scores of babies and treated hundreds of the ailing around Sheridan County in the years before a doctor ever took up residence there.

One of the earliest doctors to serve full-time in Plentywood was the youngest son of Theodore and Ruth, Gramp's younger brother Rasmus. His gravestone, of rich reddish granite, testified to his tragic early death at the age of forty. As a teenager, our father had admired his uncle greatly and while in high school Bud often accompanied the youthful doctor on house calls around the county. The two young men shared a passion for poetry and fishing and they enjoyed reciting lines as they waited for the fish to bite on their frequent trips to the pebble-lined lake north of town. They also shared a fondness for Drink, despite traditional family disapproval of such substance. They would faithfully, but furtively, patronize the taverns they passed on excursions to heal the sick or to catch fish. After his premature death a succession of other doctors came to serve the town, but Dr. Janson was always very well-regarded. People said of him, "Rasmus Janson was a great doctor, you know. Sure, he could operate better than the ones who were sober."

When visiting the cemetery Vinny liked to read aloud the lines of poetry taken from John Masefield's *Sea Fever,* which were etched delicately into the granite stone below Rasmus's name:

I must go down to the seas again, to the lonely sea and the sky
And all I ask is a tall ship and a star to steer her by...
A merry yarn from a laughing fellow rover
And quiet sleep and a sweet dream when the long trick's over

We once found a dead bird, a small sparrow with streaked feathers of white and brown, at the foot of our great-uncle's grave. We decided that it should be a companion for Rasmus to share his quiet sleep and sweet dream, and so we used rocks to dig into the soil beside his headstone, and we buried the sparrow there. On ensuing visits to the grave I always brought along an extra flower for Rasmus's pet bird.

THE SINUOUS BOX ELDER CREEK edged the eastern boundary of the community, flowing shallowly through an obstacle course of rocks before joining the mighty Big Muddy Creek south of town. Towering cottonwoods, black locusts, and box elders, some of them the original trees which had inspired the founding of the town, lined its banks. The daring boys of the town, and of course Vinny, liked to carefully balance one foot in front of the other to slowly walk across the rough-barked branches spanning high above the stream.

Although Box Elder Creek was not sufficiently deep for swimming in the oven-hot days of summer, the Big Muddy had hosted such recreation when our father was young. As it passed through dry farmland on its way to join the wide Missouri, the Big Muddy seemed less like flowing water, more like a slowly moving chocolate bog. Farm boys like Oscar and his friends could not resist its cooling potential after finishing their chores on a warm day, and they would strip off their overalls and leap in, despite the consequences. Dad enjoyed telling us, as we gasped in horror, about the time he'd had to pull thirteen leeches off his body following one afternoon of swimming.

Next to Box Elder Creek in the Old Townsite was the city park, an acre of land adjacent to the Pepsi-Cola Bottling plant and donated to the town by the owner of that company. Plentywood's swimming pool, with its concrete sides and bottom inexplicably painted a blood-red color rather than the usual aqua, took up much of the area of the park. Beside the main pool was a shallow circular basin fed by a fountain where non-swimmers could wade and splash. When Vinny and Alex were small, and I was just beginning to walk, Mother brought the three of us there to enjoy the cool waters on a scorching summer day. Much to Mother's surprise, a lifeguard ordered her to remove her daughters from the property and not return until they were decently attired. Not being able to afford new bathing suits, she had brought us to play in the water dressed only in shorts. Although our small chests were similar in every way to those of the boys splashing in the pool, we were considered to be puerile Salomes thus displaying ourselves. Our mother, who was not familiar with the unwritten dress code of the city park, tried to reason with the guard, pointing out that our bottoms were well-covered. But the rules of decency could not be compromised. Fully chastened, Mother took us home and sewed three little seersucker brassieres, garments considerably more provocative than tiny bare chests.

One time when I was a little older, three Canadians on holiday made a remarkable visit to the town pool. The occasion was memorable partly because it was highly unusual to see any adults come to swim in the overcrowded pool. Then, too, the children of Plentywood were used to recognizing all of our fellow swimmers; they were our comrades and schoolmates and their siblings and occasionally their cousins from out of town. Mostly, though, the visitors surprised us by their physical appearances—they looked very unlike all of us. When the three strangers stopped by on that hot afternoon, it was an event of great moment for that entire summer and indeed for many summers afterwards.

We knew our visitors were Canadian because rarely did any outsiders other than Canadians pass through our town. Not since the early homesteading days had Plentywood been a destination that was selected on purpose by strangers, nor was it really a crossroads on the way to anywhere else. Regina, Saskatchewan, the large provincial capital, was about a hundred miles away, and her citizens sometimes ventured south to experience American culture. On their way to other places of interest, the national parks and monuments, or cities of some size and renown, it was not unusual for travelers who had gotten a late start to spend a night at our town's one motel. And so it must have been with these visitors. After checking into the Plains Motel, which did not have a pool, the three Canadians were directed to the city park for a cooling swim.

That afternoon the pool was filled, as always, with hordes of splashing, yelling children, but suddenly there was absolute silence throughout. You could have heard a bubble burst. The Canadians, two men and a woman, had emerged from the dressing rooms and were walking across the deck to the benches upon which swimmers stowed their towels while they swam. All movement in the pool came to a stand-still as every single swimmer stared, absolutely spellbound, at the new-comers. We were not being intentionally discourteous; none of us had ever seen a human who looked anything like the trio of strangers there on the deck and we were more than a little curious. Each of the Cana-dians had black hair and very dark skin.

The woman was wearing her large beach towel wrapped around her body so that only her lower arms and her ankles and feet were exposed, and the men were partially covered by their sports shirts and the towels they were carrying. I watched the visitors intently, won-dering about their brown coloring.

Grandpa Walt's summertime skin color had always been a fasci-nation to me. When he worked at the farm Gramp wore a long-sleeved union suit under his overalls so his upper arms and chest remained the pale ivory of his natural coloring, but under the constant sunlight his hands, face, neck, and a vee shape at the top of his chest where his longjohn neck wasn't buttoned turned a deep shade of red-brown color, and it looked as if someone had painted just those areas. As I stared with inadvertent rudeness at the three strangers, I was very interested in their skin tone, imagining that it followed patterns simi-lar to my grandfather's. What I thought was that they, too, must be farmers who worked outside in the bright sunlight and they had been even more deeply colored by it than Gramp on their faces and ex-tremities. When the men removed their shirts and the lady her towel, I marveled that their skin was as brown everywhere else as it was on their faces and hands.

Children around me at the shallow end of the pool stood still and gazed as unblinkingly as I at the three, and the usual lively activity was halted all throughout the space. Somehow the visitors made their way through the intensity of our perplexed stares and silence and en-tered the pool to swim for a while, but they did not choose to stay long. Who could blame them? The situation must have seemed as dreamlike to them as it did to all of us who were there swimming on that day. We talked about the strangers long after they had gone, and their visit that summer day took on an aura of mystery and prompted a wondering among us about what other unknowns lay beyond the outskirts of our community.

A little refreshment house stood next to the swimming pool and when we had money for treats, Vinny, Alex, and I would buy banana popsicles or Black Cow caramel bars to eat in the little booths that lined one side of the deck. The booths were wooden constructions and contained two built-in benches and a small table, each of them a jackknife-carved palimpsest of initials and dates, the casual records of generations of teenage crushes. The booths were separated from each other by wildly untrimmed honeysuckle which grew up and over them to create a covering like a fairy tale thicket. This floral haven offered shade for those overheated by the sun and privacy for those overheated by their ardor. After my sisters and I ate our treats we could not swim right away under strict orders from our mother, and so we went to the playground to swing vigorously for half an hour while our food digested.

Sometimes a sudden storm descended upon us as we swam. With the first booming clash of thunder, or distant flash of lightning, all the lifeguards blasted their whistles in warning. Then,

"Storm! Everybody out of the pool!" they would shriek.

When a child was slow in responding, the warnings became more graphic:

"Hurry up! Get out! You'll be fried like on the electric chair!"

If there was no lightning or close-by thunder during a rare summer rainstorm, the pool would remain open. That was truly a fine time— swimming in the pool while a warm shower dropped gently down around you, streams of soft rain casting ripples all across the pool.

ALTHOUGH IT HAD LONG ENJOYED BEING A MONOPOLY in our town, the Red Owl Grocery nevertheless tried hard to please its customers, even catering to ranchers' needs by stocking salt licks in a variety of pastel colors and stacking them conveniently in huge pyramids by the check-out counter, just in case a customer had forgotten to pick up a few.

But now some competition came to the old wooden store when a brand new Piggly Wiggly was built of cinder blocks on the western edge of town. When it held its Grand Opening, the store with the grinning hog logo promised some great bargains, and then the established store counterattacked with its own set of specials. There arose a war of advertising between the red owl and the pink pig in our weekly newspaper. With a nagging feeling of disloyalty, but with a genuine desire to save money on her grocery bill, Mother decided one day to go shopping at the new store while Katie and Johnny took their afternoon naps. She appointed Vinny and Alex to be in charge of us younger siblings.

The toddlers were sleeping soundly in one bedroom, so we three older girls began a rambunctious game of hide-and-seek throughout the rest of the house. We played in teams, each taking a turn as the seeker of the other two, who hid together. Rules of the game required the pair to move around to different hiding places while avoiding the seeker. At one point Vinny and I were the hiders and we had secreted ourselves in the back of the hall closet. Behind the hanging overcoats in the inner recesses of the enclosure we brushed against Dad's hunting rifles which were propped up in a corner.

"We'd better move. The guns might go off," I whispered nervously.

"They're not loaded, you imbecile," Vinny hissed back. "But it sounds like Alex is down in the basement. Let's go!"

As we scrambled out of the closet, my foot kicked against the butt of one of the rifles and it fell crashing to the floor. We could hear Alex come charging up the basement stairs so we ran frantically into the bathroom and slammed the door. Alex raced after us and pounded her fists on the locked door.

"I've got you," she cried. "Locking the door is cheating."

"Quick," Vinny whispered, "out the window." She climbed up onto the counter and pushed open the high, narrow window. Then she pulled herself up to the window frame and swung her legs through the opening. With a struggle I hoisted myself up beside the sink. Vinny had her middle section balanced on the frame, arms holding her steady as she prepared to jump feet-first. Her long braids hung down by her face and she tossed them out of the way as she instructed me. "After I go, slide over the window sill, dangle your legs, and push yourself off from the wall and into the air. I'll reach up and catch you."

I didn't like the plan. I wasn't sure I was strong enough to raise myself all the way up to that high window, and if I did manage to get there without falling back into the room or right through the window, the ledge was very narrow for maneuvering into a jumping position. But mostly, the hard ground was at least eight feet below the window, and I wasn't sure that Vinny really could, or would, catch me in the air like she promised.

"I don't know if ...." I began to say.

"Sh! Come on, follow me," Vinny ordered in a bossy whisper, then pushed her body through the window. Her attempt at a silent escape ended abruptly with her ear-piercing shriek, "O-o-o-ow! Oh, help!"

I moved to the window and on tiptoe I peered over the frame. There hung Vinny, swinging madly in the air. One of her thick blond braids was caught on the window's metal hasp, and by that braid her whole body hung. Her legs were thrashing in the air and her arms flailing as she swung ridiculously a couple of feet off the ground. I pulled desperately on her braid with both hands, but the weight of Vinny's body would not allow the slightest lifting of it. I jumped off the counter and unlocked the door that Alex was still pounding hard upon.

"You've got to save Vinny! She's stuck out the window!"

Alex climbed onto the counter and quickly tried to move the braid, but she could not pull it up to slide it off the hasp either.

"Help, help," Vinny gasped, and she sounded close to tears, most unusual for the eldest sister.

"Wait, I'll go outside and lift her up. You stay here and pull her braid off the hook." Alex was showing great calm and steady judgment in the emergency. She ran outside and grabbed Vinny around the thighs and slowly hoisted her up far enough so that I could slip the thick braid off the hasp. Vinny dropped out of Alex's arms and onto the ground. She lay in the dirt for a minute or two, and I ran out of the house to see how badly she was hurt. Alex and I watched with great concern until finally Vinny sat up and began to rub tenderly with her fingers across the spot on her scalp where the braid had pulled. We two watched her sympathetically as she traced little circles through her hair. Then suddenly she was laughing. Alex and I stared at her. She roared with laughter, and each time she tried to stop she was seized with another wave of hilarity.

"What's so funny, Vinny?" we kept asking her, still too horrified by the picture of her hanging there to be able to join in her laughter.

Finally she caught her breath and stopped. "Why didn't you just pull off the rubber band to unbraid my braid, you dummies?" No one had thought of that.

ROLLER-SKATING WAS A THRILLING ACTIVITY where smooth sidewalks allowed free passage; therefore, skating could only be done in the newer areas of Plentywood. In the older section of the town, sidewalks were made of a cement composition which included stones of many sizes. The stones added an element of the natural world to the unnatural process of paving a path through dirt, but the stones also served to undermine and undo that more civilized walkway. Weakened by the extremes of temperature through the seasons, the cement paste sidewalks became brittle, cracking and dislodging the materials they were composed of. The oldest walkways were gradually reduced to mere stepping stones across shallow craters, those filled with rocks clinging to marrowish crumbs of cement.

Newer sidewalks with smoother cement surfaces were found near our family's house, but they didn't guarantee escaping without a scraped knee. Just as one of us girls was racing at full speed along the sidewalk, braids flying straight out behind, she might hit the dip of a driveway or a wandering rock in her path, and her excessive speed would help send her crashing. Our metal skates were fastened with clamps onto our shoes, tightened up with a skate key, and buckled with a skinny leather strap around the ankles. Despite the lengthy process of attaching the skates, they often loosened up quickly with the vigorous motion of skating and suddenly dragged off the shoe, tripping the skater into a major tumble. During warm weather skating days, large brown scabs covered the knees and elbows of the least skillful and the most daring of the roller skaters.

On our travels around the town we three girls often passed the man known to everyone as Two-Louse. The origin of his name was unknown, as were his actual origins. One old-timer said that Two-Louse was the son of a Frenchman called A-louse, who had been a badman at the turn of the century. If this story were in fact true, then the son more than atoned for the dirty deeds of the father because Two-louse spent all his waking hours tidying up the town. He worked his way up and down the paved streets of Plentywood, sweeping them clean with a small kitchen broom. He was never without work because the ever-present prairie winds brought continuous precipitations of light field dust to the sidewalks and roads. No one knew how long Two-Louse had been sprucing up the town. It seemed that he had always been a quiet presence on the streets. His long days in the sun had made him as brown-skinned as a farmer, and this deep coloring helped to hide clues to his age, as did the permanent thick coating of dust on his hair. He lived in a tiny shack next to the town dump, and many people thought his scavenging habit and his sweeping activity meant that he was a little bit woozy in the head.

Two-Louse rarely spoke, and when he did few people could understand him. Those who knew the story of A-louse said that when he made those queer sounds, Two-louse must be speaking some form of the French language. When children approached him, Two-Louse beamed a wide, fairly tooth-deficient smile upon them, and he always greeted Grandpa Walt in a similarly delighted fashion. Gramp must have been able to understand whatever the sweeper was expressing in his strange words, because the two men would often converse at length, much to the amazement of onlookers. Two-Louse knew that Alex, Vinny, and I were Walter's granddaughters, and so when he saw us he would set aside his broom and wave at us with both hands, fingertips slapping up and down against his palms.

But another acquaintance of Walter's frightened us terribly. We called him the 'St-St-St-Stick Man' because he carried a big wooden walking stick which he pounded heavily against the ground as he walked. He was a tall, thickset man who wore huge black-and-white striped Oshkosh overalls, similar to the small ones worn by us, and a cap like that of a railroad engineer. He may have once worked on a train, but in Plentywood his main occupation was striding around the town, always rhythmically striking his way with his stick. On the older sidewalks of our town the blows from his stick rang out with a brittle echo as he moved. The man's expression was stern, with his mouth permanently straightened into the broad line of a frown and with deep furrows in his forehead running parallel to it. His eyes were fixed upon the distance far ahead as he walked and struck at the earth. The St-St-St-Stick Man lived on the block beyond our grandparents' house so he passed by regularly. If we were playing in the yard and heard the steady pound of his stick approaching, we dove for cover beneath the honeysuckle bushes.

ONE FINE SUMMER AFTERNOON, nearly cloudless and with just a whisper of the usual prairie wind, Vinny, Alex, and I set out to visit Grandpa Walt and Grandma Christina in the older section of town. We took the train tracks for part of our journey. The worn wooden crossties were so closely spaced that my older sisters would have had to walk slowly to step on every one of them, so they were leaping over them alternately and loping along like gazelles. I moved much less gracefully as my shorter legs almost tripped on each tie as I tried to keep pace.

"Oh, there goes the Fancy Hat Lady," Vinny said. "Let's follow her."

She yanked one of Alex's arms and one of mine, and pulled us off the tracks and into an alley. The Fancy Hat Lady was another mysterious town resident, a character who might have stepped out of a Hardy Boys book. She was the most exotically dressed lady in Plentywood and she also wore the most make-up: layers of pale powder sugared across her cheeks and the brightest possible red lipstick to enflame the curves of her mouth. From a distance she appeared to be a young and beautiful woman, but at closer range her face powder could not hide the wrinkles wrapping the surface of her face like the stretched silks of a spider web. She was usually dressed in a heavy burgundy-colored cloak, no matter what the temperature might be, with the peek of a long floral skirt beneath it. And her crowning glory, above piles of henna-red hair, was the masterpiece of a hat she had selected for the day's outing. The other ladies of Plentywood wore simple, modest hats to church and civic events, small navy or pastel-colored hats which blandly cupped the top of the head and perhaps dangled a tasteful bit of netting to partially obscure the eyes of the wearer. But subtlety and coyness were not the qualities broadcast by the elaborate structures atop the Fancy Hat Lady's head. Her hats sang expressively, exotically, of Paris and Vienna, of evenings at the opera and tea in a garden or under the chandeliers of the Grande Hotel. Her hats were alive with ribbons, ruffles, feathers, and fabric flowers, and they were colored in alizarin, viridian, indigo, and violet. Her hats spread out in wide, floppily graceful circumferences or towered high above her forehead like the figurehead on a ship.

"Come on, she's heading down Dodge Street. Move it, you guys," Vinny bossed us. We walked quickly down the alley, peeking between the houses to keep the Fancy Hat Lady in sight. We had no trouble following our target. She was wearing one of the highest towering of her hats, the one Vinny had dubbed the Tower of Babel, and she was burdened with two overstuffed bags of groceries.

"Do you think she has something secret hidden under those loaves of bread?" Alex wondered. "Maybe she's a Russian spy."

If she were a spy, we considered, she might have maps of the Fortuna Air Force Base that was nearby in North Dakota, an airfield thought to harbor atom bombs. Intermittent jets flying to and from that base caused ear-splitting sonic booms to echo across the wide Montana sky, interrupting the self-contained peacefulness of a small prairie town and forcing its denizens to consider the possibility of global warfare. Even naming the base after the Roman goddess of fortune made it ominous-sounding to those who recognized the name. Would Fortune smile upon the world beyond Plentywood and help it maintain peace, or would the hiding of hideous weapons beneath the sunny prairie help unleash a Fortune of darkness and destruction? Children, too, felt the echoes of an unknown dread when startled by the sonic booms. In safety drills at school we practiced crouching beneath our desks and shielding our eyes from radiation, but this did not really reassure us, and in dreams at night some of us saw unshielded the shadow of a billowing mushroom cloud, just like the one pictured in *LIFE* magazine.

"The Fancy Hat Lady would not be a spy for the Communists," stated Vinny. "She might be a spy for our country. She could steal maps and files from the Russians and smuggle them into Washington D.C. in one of her hats or stitched into the lining of her cape."

Alex and I nodded in agreement. Vinny was always good at figuring things out.

We saw that our quarry was headed away from the central business section and into the old junkyard area of town. We passed the second-hand store with its peeling yellow paint and old china pitchers and chamber pots in the window, then next to it, an auto-wrecking yard hidden by a tall fence of vertical boards.

Through gaps in the fence we could see piles of old tires, fenders and bumpers, oil drums, and engine parts. There were also outmoded automobile frames and Vinny pointed out a drab Model T which may once have been shiny black like the one driven by Great-Grandfather Janson up until he died at the age of ninety. His son Walter liked to tell about the time Theodore had lost his temper on a family drive one Sunday afternoon when his Model T was new. This had happened in the very early days of automobile travel when there weren't many roads in the county suitable for such vehicles. After driving a great distance into the countryside Gramp's father was following a circuitous set of tire tracks through a rancher's pasture on a shortcut back to home. When he reached the end of the pasture, however, he found the fence gate closed and bolted. They had traveled many miles already on their drive, and now, with the gate locked, they would have to repeat most of the route. Theodore was furious, but in those days a true gentleman never cussed. Still, he was mad, very mad, so he suddenly leaped out of the Ford, took off his fine Sunday hat, threw it on the ground, and proceeded to jump up and down on it. Back then no one dared to laugh at his antics, and in fact his three sons were filled with fear by such an exhibition of temper, but as he told the story in later years Gramp always chuckled at the picture of his stern Swedish father stomping up and down on his best hat.

On walked the mysterious Fancy Hat Lady, she who would never abuse a hat in anger, and we three girls continued to follow her stealthily, although we were now certain of her destination. The seldom-used train tracks, busy only during harvest season when grain was shipped from the area, continued westward on their way out of town. On a dead-end track at the edge of the railyard was a wooden passenger car dating back to the early days of train travel. The former elegance of the coach was hinted at by the streaks of dark-red paint and gilded lettering barely visible on the grayed wood siding, and by the jewel-like green and gold squares of leaded glass above each arched window. Where it had originated, what exotic travels it had made, and why it had come to rest at this outpost of the Great Plains were all unknown. Inside this long-retired railcar lived the Fancy Hat Lady.

She carefully crossed the tracks with her load of groceries, a tepee-shaped woman in her wide cloak and towering hat. As she stepped onto the piled crossties which served as her front stoop, a man walked quickly around the corner of her house and joined her, then they both entered the train car. The three of us were astonished to recognize the man across the rail yard—he was Gramp's older brother Emanuel, a quiet and shy man, a lifelong bachelor who alternately blanched and blushed in the presence of females. We stood still and pondered what we had just seen. What could Uncle Emanuel possibly be doing at the Fancy Hat Lady's house? An unexpected real life mystery had suddenly presented itself.

"Well, we'd better investigate what they're up to," Vinny decided. "You stay here, Junior, and duck down behind those barrels."

I did as I was told and watched as my two older sisters sneaked over to the railcar. They climbed up onto the stoop, then Vinny bent down and held out her clasped hands for Alex to step up and peek into the uncurtained window next to the door. After a quick look she leaped down, whispered something to Vinny, and the two traded places, Alex struggling to lift Vinny up to peek in the window. Vinny got a peek, then jumped down abruptly and the two of them ran away from the car. They barely slowed down enough to grab me by the arms and pull me up, then the three of us raced out of the train yard and along the length of the wrecker's fence. I didn't know why we were running like all get-out, but I did not want to be left behind. We ran until we were well out of sight of the Fancy Hat Lady's house, then Vinny slowed down and so did we. We paused by the antique store to catch our breath. My sisters looked at each other and smiled mysteriously. I faced them.

"What was it? What did you see?" I demanded.

Vinny shook her head and wasn't going to tell me the secret.

I persisted, "What was it? Why won't you tell me?"

"Well," Alex said with amazement, "Uncle Emanuel was kissing her!"

The three of us walked along the dirt road toward downtown, then through the older streets dotted with poplars or box elders, sparse indicators that our town strove to live up to its name.

As we neared the block where our grandparents lived I scouted down the street nervously. "Do you think the dogs are out?" I asked.

"I can't see them," replied Vinny. "Let's try going this way. They must be in the house."

We walked gingerly along the crumbling sidewalk toward our grandparents' house and soon approached the neighboring yard where the fearsome dogs lived. The yard was enclosed by a wire mesh fence and had a few scraggly bushes interspersed with patches of dry grass and wide areas of bare dirt where the two worst dogs in the world had scratched and dug. The dogs were huge, ugly Weimaraners, tan in color with ghastly red-rimmed yellow eyes and fleshy, zigzagging gums surrounding their dreadful slavering mouths. They were nowhere in sight as we began to pass the yard, but with a sudden stampeding of feet and barks like the hounds of hell, the two dogs lunged out from behind a bush and charged at the fence. Growling and snarling they threw themselves at the flexible wire mesh, bending it with the pressing force of their bodies. Sheer terror shot through me. We backed off the sidewalk and began to run through the piles of soft dust which lined the road and we could hear behind us the raspy voice of the dogs' owner from inside his screen door, "Down, Killer! Down, Murderer! Down, boys! Good boys, come to Papa."

Grandma Christina and Gramp were in their large kitchen when we reached the safety of their house. Grandma was at her wooden flour table, lightly kneading a ball of dough for the crust of one of her rhubarb pies. She patted her floured hands on the full length apron covering her plaid house dress, making cloud-like white fingerprints on the blue cloth. Then she pulled open the curved metal drawer filled with flour and scooped out a small amount to dust her rolling pin. Grandma Christina's rhubarb pies were justifiably famous. She knew how to balance the almost tear-producing tartness of the rhubarb with exactly the right amount of sugar and a touch of vanilla extract. "Did you girls wipe the dust off your shoes?" she asked without turning around.

Gramp was seated at the oilcloth-covered kitchen table drinking a cup of coffee, one of his favorite at-home occupations. His cup and saucer were beige ceramic pieces decorated with cowboy brands of the Old West, and Gramp always poured his coffee into the saucer to cool it down, then he drank it directly from the saucer, plain and dark. Gramp was cooling himself down too as he sat in the kitchen, wearing just a white sleeveless undershirt with his deep-green serge trousers.

"What's the excitement about?" he asked when he saw our flushed faces.

"Oh Gramp, the dogs were going to kill us just now," I panted.

"And before that we walked by the Fancy Hat Lady's house," said Alex.

"And guess who was there?" Vinny put in. "Uncle Emanuel! Why would he go to visit her?"

Gramp looked more than a little embarrassed and his deep summer color turned even redder, but a little smile pulled at the corners of his mouth. "Her name is Jasmine," he said.

Click, click went Grandma Christina's tongue and she began speaking rapidly to Gramp in Norwegian. When they wanted their words to be private our grandparents spoke in their special Scandinavian jargon, a combination of Swedish and Norwegian understood only by themselves. What they said remained a mystery to their granddaughters, but another mystery had been solved. The Fancy Hat Lady had a name and it was Jasmine.

THE COURTHOUSE

ONCE THE COMMUNISTS had been soundly routed from the northern Great Plains during the Dirty Thirties, it was time for the socialist policies of FDR to help restore some jobs to the dispossessed farmers and others who were out of work. The Works Progress Administration temporarily revived the economy in Plentywood with the construction of a monumental new Courthouse for the county seat. It was built over a two year period and was by far the largest and grandest building ever raised in all of northeastern Montana.

When completed, the Courthouse stood solidly at the north end of Main Street and stared imperiously down the central street of the town past the four and a half blocks of businesses to the towers of the grain elevators. The three-story structure was massively square with walls of whitewashed concrete, making it resemble, our grandfather said in amusement, a gigantic salt lick with windows. The Courthouse was surrounded by the greenest lawn that it was possible to grow in that part of the world, and dark cone-shaped junipers rose up from its lushness. A rounded, whitewashed concrete wall formed a boundary of official separation from the ordinary houses abutting the county property.

On the upper floor of one of those plain houses adjacent to the Courthouse, accessed by an outside wooden staircase, was the office rented by my father, the purpose of which was proclaimed in a sign, painted by my mother, which hung over the door:

OSCAR JANSON, Attorney-at-Law

My father was not content with that humble office, however, and he was determined to move next door into the grand Courthouse building itself. A private law practice in Sheridan County consisted mostly of drawing up the last will and testament documents for elderly citizens. Of course there were rare divorce cases to handle, invariably those women who had overestimated the sociability of

Scandinavian farmers, and underestimated their longevity. This sporadic legal work was not profitable enough for our father to support a family with five children, so to supplement his income Dad joined his father in the seasonal coal distribution business. This made my father's work uniform consist of an elegant navy blue pin-striped suit and starched, cuff-linked white shirt on some days, and a blackened pair of canvas overalls with a patched flannel shirt and work gloves on others. When the opportunity arose, Dad decided to seek a more lucrative position and he threw his hat into the ring for the office of County Attorney.

Mother put her art degree to work in designing the Oscar Janson campaign posters. They were printed in a variety of pale colors and featured a good-sized rendering of our father's handsome face, this intended to help attract the voters, and particularly the female ones. On weekends our whole family went campaigning. We piled into the black Chevrolet with a picnic lunch to travel the county's paved roads and some of the main gravel ones to staple Dad's posters onto utility poles. Sometimes we saw the other candidate's poster already in place on a pole or a cluster of fence posts, and then my father just stapled his own poster above or below it to present a clear choice to the voters. In prime locations where farm and county roads intersected, there would be a whole gallery of campaign posters in many hues, advertising all of the candidates running for other offices too, those contending for Judge, Clerk and Recorder, and Sheriff.

To totally charm the electorate, colorful posters were not enough; it was necessary for candidates to make appearances at town meetings, civic celebrations, harvest fairs, and lutefisk suppers all over Sheridan County. Dad decided that if he brought along his three older daughters, we could help illustrate why he really needed the job. My sisters and I enjoyed hitting the campaign trail and riding around the countryside to the various political rallies and social happenings in the small towns, but we were not partial to wearing the dresses required for these events and it took great effort to subdue our usual energetic behavior to match the proper young lady outfits.

One Saturday afternoon Mother starched and ironed our white dotted Swiss pinafores, and we donned our best dresses, each in a special color of shimmery polished cotton——robin's egg blue for Lavinia, peach for Alexandra, and strawberry red for me. The pinafores slid on over the dresses, and Mother expertly tied huge bows with the sashes, then she sat us down to fix our hair.

Hair braiding by our mother's firm hands was unintentionally pure torture for us. First, Mother made a perfect part down the middle of the scalp, the comb working its way relentlessly through snarls like a hoe through trespassing weeds.

"Yow!"

"Hold still, dear."

Next, the girl being worked on was given half her mop of hair to hold tightly, and was admonished not to allow any strands to escape.

"You're dropping hairs in back. Hold on to all of it or I'll have to start over," Mother would threaten.

"Yes, Mommy."

After Mother divided her half of the hair into three perfectly even sections, she used water to plaster each strand into place and then she created the braid, pulling the hair so tight that the girl being worked on felt the skin around her eye and upper cheekbone tauten and she feared that her eyes would not be able to open all the way later. When the braids were both finished Mother tied satin ribbons on the ends to hide the rubber bands securing them. Our mother wore her own hair, dark auburn in color, softly waved and just touching her shoulders. She was a strikingly beautiful woman, even in the shapeless brown canvas pedal pushers she was wearing along with one of Dad's frayed dress shirts, sleeves rolled up above her elbows.

"Pretty, pretty girls," our mother told her daughters when she had finished, as if those words of sweetness could erase the memory of the excruciating pain she had just inflicted. They could.

"Now keep yourselves clean. Alexandra, make sure they don't get mussy, okay?"

Alex nodded primly. Mother always considered her to be more ladylike than Vinny and me, but in fact her knees were skinned just as frequently as ours, and she was the one who had once needed an emergency call on our doctor/great-uncle for removal of a giant splinter from her backside, an injury she had gotten by boldly sliding down a rough board at the farm.

Our father came in from the yard carrying a big bouquet of red, yellow, and white gladiolas. Each summer he planted and coaxed into glory a large flower bed at the edge of our property, cultivating an area right next to the untamed prairie. The garden contained a plethora of floral varieties in all sizes and shapes, and their many colors blazed garishly against the pale yellows and golds of the wild grasses in the fields beyond.

"I'm taking these glads to the church. Is there a coffee can to put them in?" Dad asked. We were going to campaign at a supper commemorating the fiftieth anniversary of the Medicine Lake Lutheran Church.

The town of Medicine Lake is twenty-five miles south of Plentywood near the grand expanse of water from which it derived its name. The lake is ringed in alkali deposits, the whiteness of which inspired the early settlers to assume that something medicinal and nurturing came from the salty sediments. Although they soon found that the alkali soil was as curative and fertile as that of Carthage after Roman revenge, the immense lake itself nourishes acres of cattails and attracts many types of waterfowl, making it an oasis on the dry surrounding plain.

There were already rows and rows of cars and pickup trucks spreading out in concentric circles around the church when we arrived, but at last Dad found a place to park. The Lutheran Church was built of clapboard siding and painted the customary white, and along its length were plain stained glass windows divided into grids of single-color rectangles. There was a square, open-sided bell tower above the entry doors. In its unadorned architecture and simple integrity the church resembled most churches in the county, but it was distinguished in being one of the very oldest. Dad shepherded his girls into the church.

After a series of speeches and hymns, followed by the unveiling of a dedicatory plaque, the pastor of the church invited everyone to descend into the nether regions of the church and partake of a bountiful feast prepared by the Ladies Circle. Vinny, Alex, and I were ravenously hungry after listening to all the orations and organ music, and we eagerly got into line for the food while Dad sought out some folks he had recognized and began socializing with them. As we girls picked up our plates and moved along the line, the sour smell of lutefisk wafted across the long serving table and overwhelmed our senses, making us almost nauseous with its intensity.

Our grandmother Christina was well-versed in the creation and controversy of this traditional dish. As a purebred Norwegian woman, she had served for years on the lutefisk preparation task force of the Plentywood Lutheran Church. She once solemnly explained to us the intricacies of preparing this odoriferous delicacy.

First of all, the large slabs of briny dried codfish must be broken apart with a hacksaw. Then these more manageable pieces are soaked in a lye solution for several days to reconstitute or *lute* the fish. The shingle-thin pieces puff up during this process so that they resemble the original shape of the freshly-caught fish. Grandma said that the test for proper luting was whether you could poke a finger clear through the cod at this point; you could do so only if it had swollen sufficiently.

Next the lutefisk pieces have to be soaked in plain tap water to dilute the causticity of the lye solution. There were always many opinions on the time period necessary for each of the soaking steps, but Grandma warned that the fish would become too soft for proper boiling if it were soaked too long in the plain water after being luted. The biggest point of contention between various cooks, however, concerned the time in hours, minutes, and even seconds needed for boiling the plumped-up cod. Some Norwegian chefs would boil the lutefisk only until it turned gray and glutinous, but an opposing set of gourmands insisted that the cod could be boiled longer until it lost some of its gluey texture and achieved a semblance of fishlike flakiness once again. Each group of cooks might become truculent in promoting its preferred form of authentic lutefisk, so many church suppers ended up with both varieties on the table.

Grandma said that in the golden days of lutefisk suppers, when the whole town including Catholics would attend and great quantities of the dish had to be prepared, a mighty cloud of the fishy odor would rise up from the basement kitchen and fill the body of the church, even lifting to the rafters of the choir loft. The pungent aroma, like a Pentecostal spirit, would surround the pulpit and waft through the rows of pews, and once it had permeated the entire space, its acrid presence would not dissipate for several days. My sisters and I were thankful to have missed those historic suppers.

"But anyway, why do they always have to serve lutefisk at these lutefisk suppers?" wondered Vinny. "Nobody likes it. I've never seen anyone really seem to enjoy eating it. Dad can't stand it."

Alex and I could not reply. We were both busy trying not to breathe in the fumes. We had wrinkled up our noses to make our nostrils tight slits that we hoped the lutefisk smell could not penetrate. We were not successful.

At last the line resumed moving and we passed out of range of the dreadful lutefisk and into the lovely aromas of fried chicken, baked ham, and Swedish meatballs in gravy, all of which revived our feelings of hunger. There were steaming mounds of mashed potatoes, dishes of green string beans and dishes of yellow wax beans, trays of warm, yeasty-smelling rolls, and platters of the delicious potato pancakes called lefse, some neatly cut into triangles and some more organically formed, but all displaying Dalmatian-like spots upon a cream-colored skin. In milk glass dishes square pats of butter sat on crushed ice, waiting to be spread upon the rolls and lefse.

At the end of the table there were rows of rectangular glass pans filled with green, yellow, red, purple, and orange Jello salads, their arrangement mimicking the simple-patterned stained glass windows upstairs in the nave of the church. Jello was the miracle foodstuff of the 1950's; its creative application was a culinary art. For this important celebration the ladies of Medicine Lake had gone whole hog, especially she who had added crumbled bacon to her concoction. There in the gleaming colloids were unique combinations of chopped fruits, vegetables, nut meats, and even shredded cheese suspended just below the smooth surfaces, but still visible to a Jello purist. Jello was one of my favorite foods in those days, and plain was my preference. There was a delicious summer treat Alex had ingeniously created with Jello. The recipe was simple: you put four or five ice cubes in a dish and sprinkled them with several tablespoons of Jello granules straight from a package you had sneaked from Mother's kitchen cupboard. Any flavor was delicious, but your theft was most likely to be discovered if you had taken a package of lime flavor because it dyed your lips and tongue bright green, and that evidence lasted for hours. Our mother sometimes added canned fruit cocktail cubes to her Jello salads, which was close to the goodness of having it plain, but I was truly offended by those abominations at the church supper and I refrained from taking any.

After we had heaped our porcelain plates high, the three of us found a place to sit at one of the long tables covered with white butcher paper. Dad made his way past our table, still talking to people in the crowds, and occasionally introducing us to them. "This is my eldest daughter, Lavinia," he told one well-dressed woman.

"Oh, she's a beauty with that golden hair," the woman gushed. Alex and I exchanged an amused look when we saw Vinny's bright red cheeks. We both had common brown hair and so we were used to sitting unnoticed and listening to the praises of our older sister's lovely tresses.

"She'll be breaking the boys' hearts in a few years," the woman continued.

"And that's not all she'll be breaking if the boys bother her," Alex murmured to me.

After we had eaten our suppers we lined up at the dessert table to view the variety of cakes, pies, and cookies that the church women had baked. Our favorite dessert was Norwegian krum kake, diploma-rolled wafer cookies that dissolved into sweet crumbles in the mouth. They were so light and tasty that we had to go back for second helpings. When we had eaten those, I wanted still another.

"Alex, can you come with me to get one more krum kake?"

"I don't know if we should. We're supposed to be on our best behavior, not eating like pigs."

"But look, there's a whole pile of them still on the platter. Please."

"Bring one back for me," piped up Vinny.

Alex and I boldly walked back to the dessert table where an attractive woman was replenishing the cupcakes. Her red lipstick was a little smeared; perhaps she had been sampling her wares. The woman's scarlet dress was considerably more low-cut and snug-fitting than the usual lutefisk supper garb, and it was only symbolically protected by a pert little gauze apron tied around her slim waist. "Hi, girls. What would you like?" the lady asked.

"I'd like a krum kake, please," I said meekly, pretending it was my first helping.

"Well, honey, you can have more than one," said the lady. "Sweets for the sweet." She piled six or seven krum kake tubes onto a little plate and handed it to me.

"There you go, honey," she said. I thanked her.

"I haven't seen you girls here at church before. Where do you come from?"

"We're from Plentywood," Alex said. "We're here campaigning for our Dad."

"Oh my goodness!" declared the lady. "Your dad must be Oscar Janson. He was such a good friend of mine back in high school. I was just talking to him a few minutes ago." Daddy towered above the group of people he was conversing with on the other side of the room and the woman's gaze traveled across the crowd to rest upon him. She smiled in his direction, her head tilted coyly toward one shoulder. Alex and I took the sweets back to share with Vinny.

Our father continued to work his way around the room and introduce himself to people, so we sat and played I See Something over and over again until we were sick of the game. When it was my turn to choose an object I was not at all skilled at keeping my sisters guessing for long. Once I had announced the color of the object I had chosen for them to seek, I couldn't help sneaking peeks at it, wondering whether they were about to guess it. They could follow my not-so-surreptitious glances and pinpoint my Something within seconds. Vinny, on the other hand, usually found an object so minute or distant that the other two of us finally had to give up without identifying it.

At last Dad told us it was time to go. We left the church and piled into the Chevrolet.

"Oh, Dad, can we look at the lake?" my sisters begged.

"Yeah, sure, we can," he answered and drove south a couple of miles to the shore, parking there on the gravel shoulder of the highway. We climbed out of the car and stood for a few minutes with our father, gazing at the nearly full moon shining across the wind-caressed waves of Medicine Lake.

Yesterday morning enormous the moon hung low on the ocean,
Round and yellow-rose in the glow of dawn,

Dad quoted from his favorite poet Robinson Jeffers, and to his daughters "yellow-rose" seemed the perfect description for that newly risen moon. Its bright reflections could be rose petals dropped upon the waves. After a lingering look we climbed back into the car and headed down the highway toward home. Dad was feeling pleased about seeing so many people at the church supper and he began singing a Bing Crosby tune in his fine baritone voice:

I saw those haaaaaaaarbor lights,
They only told me we were paaaaaaarting,
Those same old haaaaaaaarbor lights
That once brought you to me.

We girls loved to hear his singing, and especially the next song he launched into, *Moonlight Bay*. Dad continued with all his favorite melodies until he steered the Chevy off the highway and into the tiny town of Antelope, still about ten miles from home.

"Where are we going now?" we asked as Dad parked the Chevy in the gravel street outside the Victory Bar.

"I've got to stop in here and talk to some of the local fellows," he explained. "I want to be sure I've got their votes." He loosened the knot of his paisley necktie, slipped the tie over his head, and tossed it on the dashboard, then went out into the night. Vinny picked up the slippery silk tie and wound it around her golden hair like the headgear of a pirate.

Our father stayed in the bar for a long time. The three of us played

I See Something again for a while, but we soon exhausted the possibilities of neon lights and dim buildings as guessing objects. So then we played Monsters, a game of our own invention which involved watching for an approaching car on the highway, then ducking down onto the floor at the last moment before the yellow-eyed monster passed. We would carefully rise up again when we were sure the red lights on the tail of the monster were safely in the distance. Suspense built in between the monster sightings, and Vinny would talk about the evil deeds the monsters were planning as they amassed beyond the hillside before they appeared one by one. The more we played, the more tangible and frightening the monsters became in my mind, but this I did not reveal to my sisters. I could suffer my fear more easily than Vinny's taunting.

Finally Dad emerged from the bar smoking a cigarette and we watched its small orange glow move across the darkness until he got to the car and threw it in the gravel. As he slid into the driver's seat of the Chevy, I noticed the strong syrupy smell clinging to him, a mysterious aroma Dad always acquired when he visited taverns. He handed three little bags of potato chips to us and said, "Don't tell your mother about stopping here. She doesn't understand how these campaigns work. Okay, kiddos?"

As he pulled onto the highway, my father lit up another cigarette.

Riding through the nighttime countryside, we munched happily on our potato chips and watched the lights of Plentywood ahead, sparkling like a stretched-out string of diamonds in the dark.

THE CAMPAIGN CONTINUED on into the late summer when harvest fairs were held in many of the farming communities. The tiny town of Dagmar, only five miles from the state line of North Dakota, sponsored an election forum along with their harvest celebration. All the candidates for county offices were invited to give speeches, so Dad prepared his talk while Mother prepared us girls for attending the festival. We were wearing matching dresses of red Stewart plaid with large white piqué collars and over our braided hair, straw hats with ribbons—

boater style for the two older girls and a brimless bonnet for me that tied under my chin. My little hat also had a shiny cluster of artificial cherries on one side, crimson red and looking real enough to eat.

"Can we bring our bathing suits?" Vinny asked Dad. Beyond Dagmar and crossing the invisible border with North Dakota was our favorite place for swimming, Brush Lake. Dad said a person could swim across the lake and be right in the next state, but of course he never allowed us to try to swim so far.

"No, kiddo, we won't have time. We'll be too busy campaigning," our father said. "Alllllllllll aboard!"

Cars, pickups, and big wheat trucks were parked in a field of cut hay on the outskirts of Dagmar and people were walking on the road carrying their picnic lunches. Big brown grasshoppers zigzagged across their paths, and folks slowed their pace to accommodate passage of the frenetic creatures. There on the edge of the tiny town, the school's playground was hosting the harvest fair. A big wooden speakers' platform had been raised in front of the old schoolhouse, and all the booths displaying garden vegetables, home-canned pickles, and jams were crowded between the merry-go-round, rickety metal slide, wooden teeter-totters, and swings. Brown twine barriers had been tied across the play structures to curtail their usual use, and the swings were wound around their supporting poles and anchored high out of reach.

Our father had removed a stack of cardboard cartons from the car and now he handed one to each of us and gave us a pep talk. "You girls have an important job today," he pointed out. "I need you to pass out all of these matchbooks. You will have to smile at the people, look them in the eye, and tell them to vote for Oscar Janson. Can you do that for me?" Each box held several tightly packed rows of the matchbooks. Across the slick white surface on the front of each was written *ELECT JANSON* and on the back it said in smaller print *Democrat for County Attorney*. The party affiliation was a superfluous listing; both candidates for the office were Democrats. Republicans were scarcer than hen's teeth in Sheridan County in those days.

Dad went to take his place among the other candidates on the raised platform and we girls spread out into the crowd of people gathering to hear the speeches. Vinny and Alex moved confidently among the grown-ups, talking to them and thrusting the matchbooks into their hands. I tried to imitate what they were doing, but I soon found that I did not like this kind of campaigning at all. I was too timid to greet the strangers in a voice loud enough to be heard over the buzz of the crowd, and I was too short to catch people's attention without speaking to them. After several half-hearted attempts to pass out my matchbooks, I made my way over to the teeter-totter structure and slipped under the twine to sit down on the low end of the board. I held the cardboard box in my lap as I considered how I could get rid of the rest of the matchbooks.

Suddenly a large crewcut-haired boy jumped onto the opposite end of the seesaw and slammed his side of the board down hard. I was flung violently upward and off the board, and my hundreds of matchbooks were catapulted into the air. They rained down upon the crowd.

"Oh my," gasped several people as I and the matchbooks flew past. Then I landed smack on my backside. Many faces blocked out the blue sky above me, and many voices asked me if I was all right. I grabbed at my skirt to cover my exposed underpants, and nodded my chin to show that I was indeed all right. Then I felt someone helping me to sit up and gently brushing the dirt off my dress. My straw bonnet was hanging by its ribbons around my neck and I looked down to see that most of the beautiful fake cherries had been smashed.

"Are you okay, honey?" asked a plump lady in a pink dress. "Here, let's pick up those things you dropped."

"Oh, don't bother. I don't need them. I mean, I was supposed to be passing them out to people, anyway, except that I couldn't."

"Oh, I see," said the lady. "Well, what do we have here? ' Elect Janson'. Are you Bud's little girl?" She beamed at me.

I said yes.

"Well, sweetheart, isn't that something? I used to know Bud a long time ago. He was one of those rowdy Plentywood boys who came swimming here at the lake. And dancing. Your dad was quite a dancer. And of course our basketball team played against their team, so I would see him in the games. You know your daddy was really something, so good-looking. All those boys were, and you know they weren't named the Wildcats for nothing." She smiled as if remembering a special secret.

Bud's third daughter stared at the lady's face as she talked. It was a pretty face with very rounded, rosy cheeks and her eyes were a color I had never seen before, the rich green that emeralds must be. I knew that staring was rude but I was totally entranced by those lovely eyes.

"So, darlin', what are we going to do with all these matchbooks?" the lady wondered. "Well, I guess I can take some of them home with me," she answered herself. She brushed the dirt off of several and packed them into her commodious purse. "And don't you worry, honey," she continued, "all of us girls are sure going to vote for your daddy, and we'll tell our husbands to do the same."

I saw that most of my other matchbooks had disappeared. People had picked them up or they were buried in the soft dust and straw on the ground. I gathered up a couple of stragglers that I spotted and quickly handed them to an old man, then I skipped off to find my sisters, smiling as I thought of our father as the good-looking young man called Bud, who must have had a girlfriend in every town, considering this Dagmar lady and the one from Medicine Lake. I found Alex sitting on the ladder of the sledder-slide. She had dutifully passed out all of her matchbooks and now she held the empty cardboard box in her lap as she waited for the candidates to stop talking.

"Good work, Junior," she exclaimed when she saw that my box was empty too, and I accepted the praise, pretending that I really had passed out all of my matchbooks. I felt a little guilty about the deception but I let it go because I so much wanted Dad to think that I could campaign just as hard as my sisters. I climbed up to sit on the rung below Alex's feet. The two of us idly watched the people in the crowd. We saw that Vinny had seated herself on the wooden stairs leading up to the speakers' platform; she had a coign of vantage right in the thick of the politicking. Alex and I did not care to pay such close attention to the speechmaking. We were proud of our father for being up there on the platform, but truly, his words sounded much the same as the other politicians' words, all quite boring to us. Nonetheless, our indifference did not prevent us from fulfilling our proper duties as a candidate's daughters, and we clapped politely when each speaker ended his oration. At last the citizens of Dagmar and the farms thereabouts applauded more loudly and at length, signalling that the forum was over. Dad shook hands with the other candidates while the crowd dispersed. As our family walked back to the car Dad started laughing and said that Vinny had been a great campaigner. She had not recognized his opponent, the older man currently holding the office, and she had gone right up to him, smiled brightly, and thrust one of our father's matchbooks upon him, saying "Be sure to vote for Oscar Janson." The man had stared in amazement at the brazen girl, then he had walked over to Oscar to hand him back the matchbook and say grumpily, "I believe this belongs to you." Whenever he thought about it on the ride home, Dad chuckled like he had played a good joke on the man.

DURING THE AUTUMN MONTHS the campaign cooled down a little, along with the weather. Fewer speaking engagements were held, but both candidates continued to plaster the countryside with their colorful posters.

November came and our father easily won the election. Vinny, Alex, and I, along with Grandpa Walt, helped Dad move from his old office into the ample set of rooms assigned to the County Attorney, and the Courthouse became one of our favorite stops on our adventuring around the town. It offered many halls, staircases, and rooms for us to explore.

A visitor to the Sheridan County Courthouse enters its glistening salty white facade by climbing the wide stairs facing Main Street and then passing through heavy brass-trimmed glass doors. Such an impressive entry is required for the building which serves as repository of the county's records, those vital lists of names and numbers so briefly and finally summarizing complex and hopeful lives. The main level's spacious lobby has a floor of highly polished granite, and preserved in the hard stone is another county record of sorts in the range of tones imbedded in the granulation. The salmon, beige, gray, ivory, and black colors are found in different combinations in the boulders which continually plague the farmers' fields. During the 1950's you would cross the lobby to the right in order to enter the office suite of the County Attorney. Beyond it were the offices of the Sheriff and the Deputy Sheriff.

A large reception room connected our father's private office to the lobby, and here his secretary and a part-time clerk had their desks. We would greet those workers and then go into the vast office now occupied by our father. His room was lined with floor-to-ceiling, glass-doored bookcases that were filled with his tan-colored law books and hundreds of other tomes bound in burgundy, dark green, and brown leather. The wide oak desk and dark leather chairs around it formed a clearing in this forest of scholarly reference. I thought that if all the furniture were pushed out of the room, rowdy square dances could have been held in the greatness of the space. My sisters and I were excited to note the dimensions of the walk-in coat closet adjoining our father's office. It was so large that we were hoping to use it for a secret clubhouse.

Soon after he moved into his new office Dad hired Joyce to be his secretary. She was a local girl who had gone off to the bustling city of Billings to attend business college and there she had earned her degree in stenography. But then, terribly homesick for her home town, she had returned to Plentywood to pursue her career. Having been exposed to the more fashionable clothing worn in the big city, Joyce liked to dress in peplum-styled jackets and slim skirts with a kick-pleat in back. She even color-coordinated her high heels and handbags to each of her outfits. For a red-haired woman she was exceedingly even of temper and remarkably free of freckles, with a complexion like a porcelain plate. Her white skin was capable of blushing deep red, though, as I witnessed one afternoon when I stopped by after school to visit Dad.

On that day Joyce was not working at her desk, so I just went on into my father's office. He wasn't around, either, so I sat down quietly in his big chair behind the desk to wait for him. After sitting still for a little while, I grew restless and began to move my legs forward and back as if I were pumping myself upward in a swing. I pictured myself soaring high above the playground and so then I swung my legs at a faster tempo to maintain the height, and then the toes of my shoes began hitting the underside of the large desk with a pleasant whacking sound. Imagining that my swing was now almost even with the bar holding its ropes, I swung a little harder still, rhythmically and loudly striking Dad's wooden desk with my shoes. I had often wondered what would happen if I made a swing go higher than the supporting bar—would the force of my speed pull me right over it and wind the ropes of the swing up like thread around a spool? Would I stay on the swing if I held on tight or would the speed of the winding throw me free? Whack, whack, whack! My shoes struck loudly against the oaken desk.

"God in Heaven! What the Hell is going on?" My father suddenly emerged from the coat closet, swearing his surprise. Past him, I could see Joyce in the unlit closet, peering into the office.

"Oh, it's just Junior," my father said. "What are you doing here, honey?"

"I came by to say 'Hi,'" I answered. "Daddy, do you think I would stay on the swing, or would I be thrown off, if I pumped it so high it went over the bar?"

Joyce entered the room and I saw that she was either very embarrassed or she was coming down with a case of the measles because her lovely pale skin had turned redder than cherries.

"I don't know," my father said. "I have no idea. Well, um, Joyce and I were just looking in the closet for some envelopes, but now back to work."

He smiled. "And now you should go home to your mother, little one."

I grinned back at Dad, hoping that my cheeks were showing deep dimples like his. My father never called me "little one" any more now that I had two littler siblings.

I followed Joyce out into the reception room, noticing that the secretary had apparently not found the envelopes because her delicate white hands carried nothing. Her face was not so flushed as before but bright patches of rose still graced her cheekbones. I had a hint of a funny feeling inside my stomach, a vague awareness that something odd was happening, but I could not understand what it was.

"Good-by, Joyce." I waved at her as I skipped out the door.

DURING ANOTHER AFTER-SCHOOL VISIT to the Courthouse, Dad took all three of us daughters to the office next door to meet the Sheriff. Sheriff Ole Svengaard was imposing—a craggy-faced, big-boned man with a paunchy belly. He was fond of dressing up in the style of the Old West with cowboy boots; a sunshine yellow rodeo shirt that was trimmed in piping and displayed the big silver star of office pinned to the pocket; a black cowboy hat that he kept on even when indoors; and a tooled-leather belt and holster holding his Colt pistol, which looked like a larger version of Vinny's cap gun. But more impressive than the Sheriff's outfit was the creature he had preserved by taxidermy and suspended from the ceiling: a magnificent bald eagle. The eagle's astonishingly wide wings were stretched out as if it still hovered in flight, and it filled the vast air space of the room with the recalled memory of its movement. The dark body feathers looked a little shabby and dusty, a humiliation for such a proud creature, but its cream-colored head was majestic, the yellow beak wide open as if frozen in a scream.

Speechless under the power of such a creature, my sisters and I stared and stared until finally Vinny asked, "Where did you get it?"

The Sheriff laughed and replied, "I bagged this beauty up in Canada about fifteen years ago." Then as Dad and the three of us filed out into the hall I turned and looked back at the Sheriff's pistol, wondering if he had used that weapon, which so much resembled a toy, to shoot the eagle. I was often puzzled by the actions of grownups, but I could not begin to understand why Sheriff Svengaard had killed and stuffed that eagle.

The upper floor of the Courthouse was reached by dark gray granite stairs flanked by waxed wooden railings that were perfect for sliding upon. After making certain that no Courthouse officials were in view of the stairs, you climbed onto the railing in one of the ways you could ride a horse: either facing and straddling the wide, flat piece of oak, or sitting sidesaddle and facing out. When you let go and began to slide, either ride was thrilling and dangerous. You sailed so swiftly down the length of the staircase that it was impossible to stop yourself before the railing rounded the bend to the next flight, and the angle was such that you could not stay on the railing. If you failed to leap off quickly enough, you would find yourself unintentionally flying and your landing would be hard, right on the granite floor.

The Sheridan County courtroom occupied the full expanse of one side of the building with wide windows on the outer wall. The stately room had golden oak paneling with an impressive balustrade separating the dignity of the Judge's bench from the common area filled with rows of wooden pews for the citizen spectators. The courtroom was not frequently in use; the Sheriff apparently maintained order in the county effectively with his Colt.

The basement of the Courthouse had high ceilings and above ground windows, and it housed some miscellaneous offices and the Sheridan County Jail. A maze-like grouping of hallways led between the community of open jail cells with bars and an isolation cell behind a solid metal door. Dad had taken us girls past the jail area when we first toured the building and we had sneaked back to the basement to look at the jail cells on our own several times. Sometimes there were men in the cells with bars, and we would hurry past quickly without looking at their faces. We had also peeked through the slit-shaped keyhole of the isolation cell many times, hoping to see a really dangerous outlaw, but the room was always empty.

One afternoon when school was over, I brought my best friend Dale to the Courthouse to get a drink of water from the cold-running fountain. Dale came from a family of Swedes and she had short blonde hair, hazel eyes, and a beaming smile. On the first day of first grade I had been assigned the seat next to Dale, who turned toward me and flashed a wide smile which was missing both top front teeth. I had immediately grinned back to reveal that my two front teeth were missing also, and from that time on we were best friends. Together we had discovered the perfect secret fort inside a juniper tree at the back of the Courthouse lawn, and we would go there after school to sit and imagine adventures for ourselves while looking up at cloud patterns in the sky.

When Dale and I had quenched our thirst at the fountain, the two of us climbed the stairs to the upper floor to peek into the impressive courtroom. The tall double doors were usually wide open but that day we found them closed, so we slid down the wooden railings to the main floor to pay a visit to my father.

"Is Dad in his office?" I asked Joyce. The secretary had become very friendly, especially so toward me, and I liked her too because she resembled a movie star in her bright make-up and stylish clothes.

"No, Jeanne I'm sorry. He's in court this afternoon," she replied. Then the pretty secretary winked at us and went back to her typing, which was probably an important letter for my father. Sometimes I sat in the office while my father dictated his letters to Joyce. It was a fascinating process. His words would spill forth very quickly, a whole jumble of them at a time, as Joyce scribbled frantically on her shorthand tablet, the names and dates and actions of county business, building up into a rush that always ended abruptly with Dad saying, "Period. Paragraph." He would take a breath, or a drink of water, then again spew out words and more words, more names and cases, a whole brilliant summary of whatever business was being considered, then again "Period. Paragraph." Joyce speedily flipped the little pages of her spiral pad as she filled them up and my father continued to build his mound of words, but when at last he stated, "Period. Yours truly et cetera," I knew that the letter had ended. There was great power and finality in that mysterious phrase "Yours truly et cetera".

Dale and I walked past the Sheriff's office and down the back stairs to the basement, with me leading the way. "Come on, Dale, I can show you the jails."

"Are we supposed to go down there?" She looked a little nervous, and this made me feel smug because I knew all about the inner workings of the Courthouse.

"My sisters and I go there all the time. Anyway, the jails are usually empty. Come on."

We walked past the rows of barred cells, each one with its narrow bed and small sink, each one as empty as the one before it. Dale became more talkative, "So where are all the prisoners? There's nobody here."

"I guess no one was caught today. But I'll show you where they put the really bad guys." I led my friend down the dark hallway to the isolation cell and pointed to the white-painted metal door. "Inside this jail they keep the killers and the murderers and the burglars," I said gravely. Then I crouched down and looked through the slit of the keyhole. The cell was occupied! For the first time ever I saw that a prisoner was locked up in the isolation cell. The man was sitting on the edge of his iron cot at the far end of the room, his head bowed as if he were studying the way his hands pressed against his thighs. He was a large, dark-haired man.

"What's in there?" Dale whispered. I straightened up and my serious expression frightened Dale. "What's in there?" she repeated.

"A man. There's a man in there," I gasped, my words barely audible. "A bad guy is in there sitting on the bed. You take a look," I whispered.

Now Dale crouched and peeked into the keyhole. "I don't see anyone," she said out loud.

"SSSSShhhh! Don't talk! He's in there on the bed," I whispered.

Dale looked again and shook her head. "There's no one in there," she said quietly.

"But he was there," I insisted. "He must have moved."

I bent down to look again into the keyhole. Gazing back at me from the other side of the small opening, staring point-blank from one inch away, was the eye of the prisoner, the unblinking eye of the man who might be a murderer or robber. My body became jelly. I could not move. I was wholly hypnotized by that enormous eye staring directly into mine. If the man himself had been standing next to me on my side of the iron door I could not have been more frightened. The intense, staring eye held me in its power. The eye was magnetically fastened onto my own. I couldn't even blink. I tried to tell Dale, but my voice was locked in my throat. Moments passed and Dale tugged insistently at my arm until I somehow managed to break loose from the stare of the prisoner. I jerked my head from the keyhole and mouthed the word, "Run!" I grabbed Dale's hand and the two of us raced down the hall, up the narrow concrete stairway, and out the back door of the Courthouse, and we did not stop running until we reached the sanctuary of our juniper tree fort.

BLIZZARD

WINTER IN OUR CORNER OF THE COUNTRY was the loveliest of the seasons. When temperatures dropped the snow fell deeply and frequently in Plentywood. Sometimes it came early in October and sometimes late in May, and during the months of December and January it was a constant presence, blanketing and beautifying the bare hills and providing recreation for the children of the town.

Our family was fortunate in living right next to the golf course because it had wonderful hills for sledding. My sisters and I would spend hours gliding down the slopes, and the cold never seemed to seep through our many layers of clothing or chill our high spirits. We had a long wooden sled to share and we could all three sit on it and slide together, or two girls could lie stacked like pancakes to coast swiftly down the hills. Daredevil Vinny preferred sledding alone, not sitting up or riding on her stomach which would be easy, but instead lying on her back and blindly steering with her feet on the crossbar at the front of the sled, and she even rode standing up as on a dogsled but without the dogs. Most of her stunts ended in simple crashes in the deep snow, but one time she ran into a fence and chipped her front tooth. The neighborhood boys admired her greatly for that achievement.

During the winter after he was elected to be County Attorney, our father found a forgotten carton of his large campaign posters and he gave those to us. Alex, Vinny, and I used the unprinted sides of the colored posters for art projects, drawing and painting on them, but then it occurred to us that the slick printed sides might be useful in the snow. We carried a stack of the posters over to the golf course and tried them out on the longest slope. With the slippery side down on the snow, and the passenger sitting in the middle of the poster and lifting up her legs, the low-riding conveyance made for a faster, bumpier ride over the golf course moguls. Each poster made several trips down the hill before finally shredding apart.

In a corner of our grandparents' basement Vinny found another means of transport over the snowy slopes—our father's old-fashioned skis. They were hand-carved out of light-colored wood, and were about eight feet long with leather straps and buckles to bind them to the skier's boots. Vinny soon mastered the art of skiing, crouching low as she set off down our favorite sledding hill, then raising herself to standing. She became adept at coasting down the full extent of the running hillside, using nothing but her body to balance her downward movement, letting the long skis carry her smoothly to the flat expanse at the bottom.

"You try it, Junior," she urged me one afternoon, having taken several runs herself.

"The skis look sort of big for me," I demurred.

"Oh, they're big for me too, but you just slip your boots into the leather slots and I can tie the straps to make them fit."

"Well, they look kind of long, I mean."

"Skis are supposed to be long, Silly. Hey, you know what I think? I think that you're too scared to try them."

I thought of how easy it looked when Vinny glided down the hill. Maybe I could do what she did.

The two of us picked up the skis and trudged up the slope. At the top I stood nervously while Vinny tightened the leather straps around my red rubber boots and knotted the extra lengths securely. The curved-up tips of the wooden skis stretched far, far out in front of my boots, and beyond them the long hill seemed to drop off much more steeply than when I looked down it while seated on the sled or a campaign poster. I was totally terrified.

"Here, I'll get you started," Vinny said. She reached out with her fingers spread wide and pushed firmly upon my back. With that shove, the skis slid forward, slowly at first, then they picked up momentum and glided swiftly over the steepest fall of the hillside. I felt the thrill of speed in my flight and at the same time a surprisingly solid connection to the heavy skis as I held my skinny legs steady. There was a flatter stretch of the hill midway down, and the skis slowed a little as they passed over it, but then they raced fast and smooth again across the lower stretch of the hill.

It was truly a joyous ride after all. I was gliding like a hawk in the sky. But oh! my ecstasy was fleeting. As I neared the bottom of the hill, a pack of neighborhood dogs came out of nowhere to surround me and leap excitedly in front of my flying skis, all the while barking boisterously. I was terrified of charging, barking dogs because I was sure that their probable purpose in life was similar to that of Killer and Murderer, namely, to chew my body into mincemeat. Flashes of yellow pointed teeth and long, eager tongues threatened me from every direction. Many shades of hairy legs scrambled back and forth in my path. Now panicky tears ran down my face as I tried to hold my shaking legs straight enough to ride the skis through the mob of cavorting dogs. I thought that surely one would jump up and bite me, or another would leap directly in front of me and trip me off the skis, and then the whole rough gang could rip me apart as I lay stuck in the snow.

All at once a bombardment of snowballs flew around me as Vinny came running and stumbling through the deep snow of the slope, pelting the dogs as she came. Mercifully she was able to distract them and drive them off. I crossed the flat field at the bottom of the hill and coasted to a stop, remarkably still upright on the skis. I had managed to traverse that long hill just as skillfully as Vinny, and while traveling through a pack of crazed dogs too. Vinny tossed her last snowball at me. "You looked so funny in the middle of all those dogs," she said.

AN ESPECIALLY HEAVY SNOWFALL produced a solid foundation for constructing forts and snow sculptures. The weight of the accumulated snow packed the lower level even more densely, and though successive layerings of feathery snow fell from the sky, Vinny knew how to excavate from the bottom of the snowpack the thick, crusty blocks suited for building walls. On one opportune day, she used Dad's shovel to dig up several such chunks of snow and put Alex and me to work transporting them to the edge of our yard. There she had tramped out a six by four foot rectangle with her boots, the traced plan for a snow fort. We packed our blocks closely together along her boundary, filling in the gaps with handfuls of loose snow. A narrow doorway was left on the side facing our house. Then, more digging, more hauling, and a second level of the oversized white bricks, then a third and a fourth made the walls of the fortress sufficiently high for us girls to conceal ourselves in a snowball fight. Neighborhood boys liked to throw extra hard snowballs, some meanly formed over rocks or ice cubes, and Vinny wanted to be able to fight back at them from behind a substantial barricade. When the fortification was completed, Vinny ordered that a supply of weapons be concealed inside, and we three packed dozens of snowballs and piled them in the fort's corners. We were ready for warfare.

Daylight was fading, and our father's car pulled into the driveway. We proudly showed Dad our fort and cache of materiel, and he voiced his approval. The four of us stomped the snow off our boots and went inside our house, and there the hearty aroma of supper, scalloped potatoes and meat loaf, reminded us that we were starving. Spending the afternoon in the cold outdoors produced a specially deep kind of hunger.

During the night it snowed again, continually and excessively, and the northwesterly wind blasted the snow into deep drifts that enclosed our house. When we awoke the next day our raised bedroom windows were completely covered over in white, with not even an inch of the sky in view. Vinny dressed quickly and rushed outside. She saw that the front door had been blocked by an undulating wall of snow which continued all along the length of our house, but Dad had cut a path through it to reach his car. She followed the narrow trail through the cliffs of white and she saw that on the western side of the house the snow banks reached over and continued onto the roof. She looked for the walls of the fort that she, Alex, and I had spent all of the previous day building, but they had disappeared. Great rolling piles of snow filled the yard and continued out into the prairie beyond, and she knew that underneath one of those piles was our hard-worked fort and at least a hundred snowballs.

After breakfast, under a brilliantly clear sky, the three of us dug out a tunnel through the dazzling white snow. The heat radiating from our house had pushed the drifts a small distance away from its outer walls, as if asserting on our behalf an innate human resistance to the excesses of nature. Vinny took the shovel into the open space beside our house and she began to scrape out a passage into the drift. When she had formed the opening at the bottom, she climbed up on the drift and began to dig her way down. After a while Alex relieved her at wielding the shovel, and the two, aided a little by my eager attempts to help, gradually dug out a sloping tunnel. Vinny tried it out, and it was just barely big enough for her to fit through. She tamped down the bottom of the tunnel with the shovel and tried it again. It was now easier to fit through, but the sliding was still too leisurely for Vinny's purposes. She fetched a bucket of water from the basement, then another, to pour down the hard-packed floor of the tunnel and when it froze, very quickly in that cold, she had an ice slide. She tried it again, lying on her back with feet first, and she found that the slide was so slippery that it was impossible to stop at the bottom before slamming hard into the side of the house. More arduous work with the shovel created a long curve to the tunnel, turning it away from the house, and when she iced the surface, her incredibly slick tunnel slide became a thrilling ride that attracted all the children from blocks around.

When the conditions were right, with a little moisture in the usually dry snow that fell over the prairie, children formed snowmen out of the billowing piles of white covering their yards. One winter day, with the sun glowing and the temperature not especially frigid, Mother thought that we should build a snow sculpture in our front yard. A snowman was too common as subject matter and so we all decided we would construct a snowhorse.

Mother had always been fond of horses and in her artwork she often used images of them. As a girl she had collected equine figures in many sizes and materials from the various countries she had visited. She had several small ceramic horses from China, each one in a different color and pose. They were kept on the top shelf of the bookcase, safely out of reach of the toddlers, and we bigger girls were constantly creating new arrangements for the herd. On that afternoon we studied them carefully before deciding that it would be structurally most practical to copy the one that was in a resting position, legs curled up below its body. The figurine was about two inches long but we planned to make our snowhorse life-size.

Mother tucked Katie and Johnny into their beds for naps, then she, my older sisters, and I bundled ourselves up and went out into the snowy yard. We set to work energetically and the snow was of such a perfect quality for building that the bulk of our animal rose up quickly from the white surroundings. With all four of us pulling in and packing down armloads of the moist snow, we soon saw that the rectangular base from which our horse's form would rise had far exceeded our initial plans for making it life-size. Our mound was shaping up at nearly three times the size of a normal horse's body. It was still rather shapeless, lacking the head and the characteristic curve of the animal's back. Mother supervised the four of us as we finished delineating the folded legs, and then she divided the group for the rest of the sculpting. She and Alex would form the neck and head of the horse, and Vinny and I would carve out the curve of the back and build up the haunches and tail.

Periodically Mother popped her head inside the front door to listen for the babies waking up, but Katie and Johnny tended to sleep soundly in cold weather, like little bear cubs in the warm den of their blankets.

When the giant equine form was near completion Mother stepped back for a better view of our artistic endeavor. She gazed at the frigid sculpture for just a moment, then her studied expression crumpled into one of mirth, and peals of laughter rang across the snowy yard.

"What's so funny?" we asked.

But Mother was overcome. We had never seen our mother laugh like that. She laughed so hard that she reeled back, her boots slid on the packed-down snow, and she fell right onto her backside, luckily into a good-sized drift. Landing in the soft snow made her laugh even more.

"Mommy, what's so funny about our horse?" we demanded.

"What horse?" Mother finally gasped. "All I see is a big, fat camel."

Vinny and Alex pulled our mother up out of the snow, then we all stood still and looked at our masterpiece, our wonderful creation that was meant to be a snowy white stallion. Alex and Mother had flagrantly exaggerated the curve of the neck on the animal, and its snout was too squarish and not conical enough for a horse, and the ears were too short. For our part Vinny and I had not removed enough snow from the mid-back area of the animal to give it enough of the characteristic downward curve which could rise into the rounded haunches of a horse. All in all, it certainly was not a horse but indeed the beginnings of a camel resting there in a vast Sahara of snow. So we set to work to fix our misshapen beast.

In late afternoon the four of us were still smoothing out the huge mound of the camel's hump when Dad's black Chevrolet arrived in the driveway. He got out of the car, looked our creation over, and exclaimed, "Well, that's unusual…..a giant snowcamel!" So it was.

ON COLD WINTER NIGHTS, sometimes 40 degrees below zero on the northern plains, when a lonely wind came moaning through the hills, our father liked to take his book of Robert Service's poetry over to the hearth and read aloud to his family:

> *There are strange things done in the midnight sun*
> *By the men who moil for gold;*
> *The Arctic trails have their secret tales*
> *That would make your blood run cold;*
> *The Northern Lights have seen queer sights,*
> *But the queerest they ever did see*
> *Was that night on the marge of Lake Lebarge*
> *I cremated Sam McGee.*

The Northern Lights appeared at special times in northeastern Montana, glowing mysteriously beyond the hills facing Canada. Sometimes they formed curtains of emerald and scarlet against the dusky sky, and sometimes they were ribbons of salmon pink dancing in swirls across the night. And, more rarely, the aurora borealis became a ghostly bride with a long white wedding veil arching down from the dome of the sky and spreading out to brush softly over the dark hills.

One evening after supper, while Alex helped our mother put the toddlers to bed, Vinny and I sat quietly reading in front of the fire. All of a sudden Vinny got up and started putting on her outdoor clothes. "Come on, Junior, we're going outside," she said resolutely.

"But it's freezing cold out there, probably 20 degrees, Dad said. And besides, I'm at a good part in my book. Billy Possum is trapped in Farmer Brown's henhouse."

"Billy Possum will get away. Put on your coat, Junior Fraidy-cat. I want to show you something."

It was never wise to defy Vinny's wishes; I had never successfully done so. I bundled myself up and we headed out into the frigid night. Vinny led the way around the deep snow drifted up beside the house and then out into the open field beyond our property. Plowing through the piles of snow by lifting our knees high, we made our way into the obsidian night, heading further and further away from the lights of our warm house. The air was intensely still, and the great silence was interrupted only by the muffled rustling of our boots through deep dry snow. It seemed to me as if we had become the only creatures left in a world of soft whiteness. The clear dark sky, glassy, was its opposite. In the middle of the field Vinny finally stopped, she looked around at me, and then she dramatically dropped herself backward into a giant snowdrift. "Lie down here," she told me.

"Right in the snow?"

"Yes, you'll see." She reached for my mittened hand and pulled me down onto my back. We lay quietly in the freezing cold pile of snow and stared up at the millions and millions of twinkling diamonds in the black night. The sky was impossibly huge and there had never been so many stars before. They were endless; they sparkled into eternity.

The snow cushioned like a downy comforter beneath us, and though well-ensconced in the snowbank, we began to feel warm. We were completely entranced by the magical beauty above and around us, and the two of us lay there for a long time without speaking or moving. I felt such a burning glow of deep happiness inside me that I wondered how so small a body as mine could contain all the joy given to me by that vast and radiant sky.

We had no idea how many minutes we spent there. It seemed like we could have lain there all night long, but at last the spell was broken. We began to hear indistinctly, and then more clearly, our father's voice calling out our names into the night, a solemn tolling across the drifts of snow: "LA-VIN-I-A, JE-EANNE, LA-VIN-I-A, JE-EANNE". Over and over he called until that insistent summons could not be ignored. Reluctantly, we pushed ourselves up from the bed of snow and trudged back through the field, now lifting our knees more slowly, dreamlike, as we traveled toward the shining beacon of our porch light and inside the house, our ordinary wooden beds.

SOMETIMES THE EARLY MORNING LIGHT through our high bedroom windows was softened into a silvery diffusion as it passed through a thick coating of frost. I would climb up onto the bookcase headboard of the big bed I shared with Katie to get a closer look at the feathers, flowers, and paisley delicately etched in ice on the glass. With my finger I followed the flowing shapes, not touching them but tracing them in the air and feeling a wonderment at their intricacy. As my warm breath made the frozen cover more yielding, I might scrape my fingernail across the pane, making a shirred trail through the plumose patterns. I once tried licking the little gratings of ice from my finger but I found that Jack Frost's special sherbet tasted merely of dust.

Icicles formed off the eaves when the bright sun blazed over our snowy roof and caused a temporary melting. The smaller ones looked like crystalline carrots, and we considered them to be as edible as the orange type. When the snow banks were high enough to give her a boost, Vinny reached up and broke off the pendent pieces of ice for Alex and me to suck on like lollipops. The giant icicles which collected near the corners of the house and sometimes lasted for weeks were considerably more ominous. Grandma Christina had told us of a little boy who played under just such an icicle and was fatally conked by it when it suddenly dislodged. We observed the growth of the largest of the icicles warily, watching them become thicker and longer from day to day, changing from daggers into huge swords, and we kept our distance to avoid their deadly possibility.

The children of Plentywood walked to school in all kinds of weather, and this necessitated bundling up in several layers during the coldest days of winter. Girls would pull on snowpants under their dresses, woolen socks over their shoes before putting on their rubber boots, and sweaters, coats, caps, mittens, and scarves. The temperature was often well below zero in the morning as we left home and my sisters and I had a long walk from the edge of town. When I stepped out the front door in such weather the sudden shock of cold air stabbed cruelly into my chest and I felt like all my breath was being sucked right out of my body. I would have to take several slow, tiny breaths until the air became less painful and I could move through it, and then I would have to hurry across the buried yard to catch up with my sisters, stepping into the footprints they had already pressed down into the thick white covering.

With the snow piled up in high banks along the side of the road, mounds first created by a snowplow and then added to by northerly winds, it was often necessary to walk down the middle of the street to get to school. Snow was drifted up against the houses too, and it completely covered bushes and small juniper trees, making a smoothened, softened world of white to pass through. If new snow was falling as we walked, we opened our mouths to feel the flakes tickle our tongues and we watched them touch down on our coat sleeves to create lacy designs across the wool. When the sun peered through the gray clouds in between snowstorms, it dazzled with an icy luminosity, not powerful enough to cause a melting in that freezing cold, but bright enough to sparkle across the drifts like fairy dust.

ICE-SKATING WAS A POPULAR ACTIVITY for Plentywood citizens of all ages. When the temperatures dropped low in the autumn, a large, embanked vacant lot was repeatedly flooded and frozen until a solid rectangle of ice at least a foot thick covered it, transforming the lot into the municipal skating rink. There was an old shack beside the rink, fitted with an antique pot-bellied woodstove kept so constantly stoked by skaters that its metal belly glowed orange-red and blasted out enough heat to satisfy even Sam McGee. Wooden benches lined the walls of the shack where people could sit down and take off their shoes and boots and put on their heavy woolen socks and ice skates. The wooden floor of the hut was rutty with the gashes made by hundreds and hundreds of skate blades over the years as the skaters hobbled their way to the door, before bursting forth freely onto the ice.

The volunteer caretaker of the ice rink was our grandfather Walt. He loved to skate and he moved solidly and gracefully over the ice with his hands clasped behind his back, legs crossed like scissors around the curves, a broad smile beamed at the other skaters. Gramp kept the little shack stocked with freshly chopped wood for the fire, and whenever a snowfall heaped its soft covering over the ice he got out a wide snow shovel and skated his way back and forth across the length of the rink, depositing piles of the feathery snow over the banks. Children lined up behind him, each clasping the person in front by the waist, and a long caterpillar of skaters eagerly followed the cleaned-off path as Gramp plowed it. He brought bulging pocketfuls of salted-in-the-shell peanuts to share with all his young friends and he was so popular among the children of Plentywood that they, too, would have elected him mayor of the town.

Nighttime skating was lovely on the vacant lot. A single street light at one end glowed softly over half of the ice, and deep shadows reposed on the other half. Snowdrifts around the banks delineated the boundary of the rink for those bold skaters venturing into the darkness, and the quiet of the shadows was pierced harshly by the slashing of their skate blades. On clear nights when a bright moon was shining, the whole rink glistened like frosted glass, and many skaters left their warm homes to glide and circle beneath the midnight blue canopy.

ONE AFTERNOON THE SNOW was falling hard when school let out so I walked over to my father's office in the Courthouse. My usual walking companion, Dale, was at home sick with the measles, and I did not feel like battling my way through the wind-driven blasts of snow by myself. Alex and Vinny would not be dismissed from their classes for another hour and it was much too cold to wait for them on the playground. As I crossed the Courthouse grounds, I noticed that the upper walls of the huge white building were disappearing, being swallowed into the light snow-filled clouds.

Inside, I saw that Joyce was not at her desk, nor was my father in his office, so I sat down at the clerk's desk to wait. After remaining still for a few minutes, I became restless and began looking through the drawers for something to occupy me. I found a boxed set of rubber stamps that I liked to play with, stamps of different shapes used on official documents to illustrate how traffic accidents had happened. The stamps included embossed forms with parallel lines to lay out the streets, little crossed shapes to show intersections, arrows to indicate direction of movement, and various vehicles including cars, trucks, trains, and busses, all pictured from above to create an accurate aerial lay-out of an accident. From another drawer I got out a stamp pad and the unlined sheets of yellow paper that I was allowed to use for drawing and I began creating my own maps of traffic. I made several, then I added elaborate border designs around them. I was so involved in stamping my patterns that I didn't hear my father come through the door connecting the Sheriff's office.

"Well, look at the new clerk!" Dad exclaimed. "Glad to have you working for me."

Then, glancing at his watch, "Why didn't you walk home with your sisters, Junior? The Sheriff says they let school out early because the snow's getting so heavy."

"Oh, I didn't know they were out already. I came over to ride home with you."

"Well, that's fine, but I need to finish up a few things in my office before we go."

I moved my chair closer to the cast iron steam heater and I watched the falling snow through the high windows. Thicker and thicker it came pelting down, making me dizzy to watch it. Soon I couldn't distinguish the snowflakes from the space behind them; it was all a blurred, whirling mass of whiteness. The reeling motion transfixed me until I felt as giddy as Alice falling down the rabbit hole. "It's really, really snowing," I mused to the empty room.

At last my father called from his office, "Time to go, kiddo". I came to the door and watched him pulling his wraps from the coat closet. He wound his wool scarf around his neck, then put on his big black overshoes, heavy tweed overcoat, leather gloves, and finally his elegant gray fedora. Then Dad and I took the back stairs down to the parking lot behind the Courthouse and we got into the black Chevrolet. It was the only car left.

My father could barely see through the deluge but he was able to follow the low hedge along the driveway to pass out of the Courthouse grounds and across Main Street onto the long road leading toward home. There was so much snow already on the street that he was driving very slowly, but still the car was sliding sideways every few yards as it plowed through the ever-deepening piles. Furiously swirling flakes came at the car from all angles and the violent, abruptly changing wind beat against its sides. The sky itself seemed to bend down closely over the car, a felted blanket of heavy whiteness which seemed like it wanted to smother us.

Dad kept the car centered by following the banked-up drifts lining the road from previous snowfalls and plowings. He had some trouble seeing the streetlight poles along the way but he tried to keep track of how many we were passing until he figured we had reached the large block of land occupied by the county hospital. On the other side of the hospital property was our house, the last dwelling before the hills of the golf course met the wide empty prairie. Dad turned the car carefully around the street corner that he was not really seeing but was judging to be there by the dim opening between the drifts. Then he drove slowly along what he guessed was the periphery of the hospital property. As we crept along it seemed like our black Chevy was gradually being swallowed into a ghostly cave and finally everything was blocked out of view by the pressing white walls.

The car's motion slowed more and more until it felt unreal, as if we were traveling in a dream, and then it stopped completely. Dad pressed on the gas but the tires spun in place, then he tried to go in reverse and still they spun.

"Damn it to hell," he said softly. "Stay in the car, Junior. I'll be right back."

As I sat alone in the big front seat of the Chevy, I listened to the roar of the blizzard that was muffled only a little by the surrounding walls of snow. I had never heard a blizzard wind so close before; I was always safely indoors when they hit. This wind was bellowing and howling like a tremendous beast, if not hundreds of them—grizzly bears and wolves.

I looked in amazement through the windshield at what was becoming a very thick covering of snow pressing down on our car. I wondered if Dad and I would have to dig a long tunnel under the piles of snow to reach our house. When my sisters and I had built the snow tunnel in our yard, it had taken us most of a day. Considering that, and the fact that we had no shovel with us, my father and I would never be able to dig a tunnel fast enough through all of that snow to make our way home in time for supper. I was beginning to feel hungry.

It seemed that my father had been gone for a long time. I saw that the space around me was now bathed in a grayish yellow light, a light like nothing I had ever seen before, strangely dull and bright at the same time. That kind of dark glow seemed to be coming from beyond the snow which covered our car, from up above it where the sky should have been, where it had been before it disappeared into the storm. For some reason that I cannot clearly grasp even now, I was not afraid of that blizzard. The roaring, howling, screaming of the wind, though close-by, seemed very far removed from me as I sat in the front seat of the familiar old Chevy. And the mysterious quality of the light permeating the packed snow was both fascinating and comforting to me.

Finally I heard a rough scraping and Dad appeared through the whirling snow at the passenger side door. He yanked the door open and a torrent of snow blew onto the seat. A mighty blast of wind tore through the car as he grabbed my arms and pulled me through the door. He bundled his big arms around me and carried me through the driving snow and wind and magically, it seemed, right into a warm house. There he set me down and told me what had happened. When he left the car he discovered it was wedged firmly into a snowdrift and he tried to dig it out with his hands. He soon determined that was impossible so he tried to figure out exactly where we were. As he struggled through the drifts he sank down into the hedge of the Hansen family's yard. He pulled himself out and then oriented himself by the layout of the hedge to figure out where he could find the front door of their house through the blinding snow. Then he returned to the car to get me.

No one was home in the Hansen place so Dad tried to use their phone. "Hello!" he yelled into it repeatedly but there was no answer from Agnes.

"Damn. The phone line's dead. Now we can't call to find out if Vinny and Alex got home okay." Dad looked worried as he considered the possibilities. "Junior, I'm going to have to leave you here by yourself. I've got to get to our house and see if your sisters made it home before the storm picked up. There's no way I can carry you with me through these winds but you'll be fine until the Hansens get back." He winked at me and then went out into the blizzard.

I felt just like a brown-haired Goldilocks uninvited in the bears' cottage. I was feeling quite hungry but Mother had always told us that it was exceptionally bad manners to look in the cupboards or refrigerator of someone else's house so unlike the other intruder, I didn't go snooping for food. Instead I pressed myself into one corner of the sofa and picked up a *National Geographic* from the coffee table. I flipped through the magazine but I could not focus on the wonderful, exotic pictures. The incessant howling of the winds would not let me concentrate as I thought of my father pushing his way against them.

After Dad left me in the house he made his way back to the car and tried to estimate the angle he would need to follow from the Hansens' yard to reach the hospital. With no visibility at all through the rampaging storm, he knew that he would need the long brick wall of the hospital to guide him toward our house. Struggling against the violent winds which had quickly robbed him of his wool hat, Dad set out through the shifting banks as the dry, hard snow slapped against his cheeks and sliced at his eyes. Although he was a tall man of athletic build, he advanced slowly against such an angry adversary, and he was knocked off his feet several times by the harsh gusts. Finally, though, he bumped into the brick surface of the hospital wall. Bracing himself against it and feeling grateful for its distinguishably rough texture, he moved slowly along its length. That was the easy part of his journey. At the end of the wall he needed to throw himself into the direct force of the brutal north wind and fight his way blindly across the fluctuating space to get to our house. If the fierce wind changed suddenly again and buffeted him out of the path he was visualizing only in his mind, he might miss the house completely and wander out into the open fields. He would have no way of finding his bearings until the blizzard ended, and by then it might well be too late for him.

Oscar Janson was not a deeply religious man, despite his frequent appearances at church lutefisk suppers and Lutheran services on Sunday morning, but it may be imagined that on this occasion as my father threw himself into the hellishly raging blizzard he prayed for all he was worth. Whether prayers were answered or his own determination was sufficient, at last my father succeeded in wresting his way across the broad surrounding property of the county hospital and up to the far corner of our house. Another three or four feet in the outside direction, a length beyond the stretch of his arm, and he would have missed the corner of the house completely and wandered unseeing into the vast emptiness of the prairie. Somehow he had made his way home, losing only his favorite hat on the way, and he found his two older daughters were safe and warm and already eating supper.

I was soon rescued from my hunger and solitude by the return of the Hansens. They were astonished to find me in their living room but they welcomed me warmly. I was fed a hearty supper of macaroni and cheese, given a warm bath with the daughter closest to my age, and tucked cozily into bed with her, wearing her spare pajamas. I lay quietly beside her before I fell asleep, still thinking of the ferocious power of that blizzard. I could hear its loud wailing, unrelenting in the dark, but I sensed through the winds and snow separating us that all was well with my family.

And as it turned out, the gray fedora miraculously survived the blizzard too. A farmer found it the following summer in his field fifteen miles away, and when he read my father's name printed inside the band, he returned the hat.

CIRCLES

SPRINGTIME BROUGHT WARMING WINDS to shrink the leftover piles of dirt-speckled snow and to spread an air of fresh earthiness through our town. With the gradual melting, squishy swamps appeared in streets, yards, playgrounds, and verging fields. The almost liquid mud slowly curdled into a thick fudge, then it flattened out and cracked into honeycomb-shaped segments that curved upward at their edges as they stretched into dryness.

With winter's ground sufficiently solidified, it was time to play marbles. Schoolboys loaded up their jacket pockets or marble bags and brought their prize shooters to school. Before the opening bell, during recess times and noon hour, and after school was dismissed, boys challenged each other and crouched in the dirt to play out their contests.

Girls usually spent their playtime tossing balls against the brick walls of the school or jumping rope on the sidewalks, but my friend Dale and I found those activities humdrum and we much preferred to play marbles with the boys. Each of us had a marble bag made of purple velveteen cloth with *Seagram's Whiskey* embroidered on it in gold thread and with a thick golden cord you could use to dangle the bag from your wrist. The bags had been wrappings for bottles of whiskey purchased by our fathers, and they were perfect for carrying our marbles to school.

Marbles were valued for their color, size, unique markings, and history of having good luck in challenge games. They were collected, haggled over, and traded like small treasures. There were four types of marbles: peeries, cat eyes, plains, and steelies. Peeries were considered to be the most valuable. They were clear glass in a single "peer" (pure + clear) color which could be red, amber gold, green, no-color/see-through, aqua, or sapphire blue. The peeries had tiny air bubbles inside the glass and they looked like jewels when held up to catch the light of the sun, especially the reds which turned into brilliant rubies. Cat eyes were clear glass marbles with a twisted strand of two or three colors in the center and they could be very pretty if the colors were harmonious. The plains were opaque glass with one to three colors swirled into the surface. Some of them resembled the planets, which I'd seen pictures of in *The National Geographic Magazine*, and others were like little landscapes of fields and roads or colored clouds against a pale sky. The steelies were just balls of steel, industrially ugly and not part of most girls' collections.

There were four sizes of marbles and we called them boulders, biggies, regulars, and teenies. Boulders were the largest, and they were usually plains or steelies; peerie and cat eye boulders were rarer and therefore highly prized. The next size we called biggies and those marbles were about three-quarters the size of boulders. The regulars were the variety used most often in games, and then there were the under-sized marbles, always peeries, which we called teenies. I thought of the teenies as the baby children of the boulders. I liked to spread out my whole marble collection on my white bedspread and sort them into little groupings of size and color. The lumps and depressions of the bed made a landscape of hills and valleys to separate the various marble families and tribes, and the furrows of the chenille fabric created roadways along which to roll them.

Vinny was a champion marble player with a collection that rivaled that of any boy in town. Vinny's collection measured six inches deep in a cardboard grocery box and contained hundreds and hundreds of the colored orbs. She kept her steelies in a separate shoebox so they would not chip the glass marbles. Except for the steelies, I hoped to have such a collection myself someday.

Two varieties of marble games were played by our town's children. The first was a simple challenge game between two players which was sometimes preceded by a great deal of bargaining as to which size and type of marble would be used in the game, and what the stakes were for the contest. Boys often bet several marbles on the outcome of a single game whereas the girls preferred to bet only one marble, and one that was not especially pretty or proven to be lucky. When the terms had been settled the game began with the first player, the one who had been challenged, shooting the marble as far as possible by flicking it out of a rolled fist using the thumb. The second player's marble went in pursuit, chasing the first around the irregularities of the ground, past rocks and weeds, through grass, and over sidewalks. The two players continued to alternate turns, taking shots at each other as they traveled over the terrain until at last one marble struck the other solidly enough to make a clacking sound and move the opposing marble visibly. The crowd of children watching the play served as judges of fairness and they were quick to call "dragging" if a player sneakily pushed a marble rather than flicking it cleanly with the thumb. The loser of a challenge forfeited the stake to the winner.

The second game could be played by several children at once. A large circle was drawn with a stick into the playground dirt. Players positioned themselves around the outside of the circle and in turn each shot a marble into the center. The play continued clockwise around the periphery as each person tried to eliminate another marble by hitting it solidly. A hit marble was removed and given to the player who had struck it, and the game continued until a final shooter had eliminated the last competitor with a clean hit to take that marble. Another version of the circle game had all the hit marbles removed from the circle and collected together as great booty for the last remaining player. A fortune in marbles could be accumulated or lost during recess.

Even before the mud dried up and the days became warmer, eager children swarmed over the play equipment during recess and noon. Most had not played on the metal structures during the coldest days of winter when the bars were too frigid to touch with bare hands, and too slippery for mittens to grasp. When the weather was extremely cold, older children—mean ones—sometimes dared younger students to try tasting the frosted surface of the metal bars. A bloody tongue ensured that we who were foolish enough to take the dare did so only once.

The swings were suspended on very long ropes from an iron A-frame structure. Their wooden seats were wide enough for two children to share in the usual situation of there being more swingers than there were swings. One person stood and straddled the seated friend, and both riders pumped their legs hard to soar as high as possible into the air. When there was a dearth of swings Dale and I often shared one, and the two of us were very efficient pumpers. When we did get to have individual swings we would compete to see who could pump herself up the fastest to be even with the top of the monkey bars nearby, and we would hold another contest to see who would dare to bail out of the swing from the greatest height. I excelled at the latter feat, to which my constantly scraped knees testified, as well as my eventual perfectly flat feet.

Dale and I were also fond of the monkey bars for performing various acrobatics. We could swing like chimpanzees from bar to bar, twist ourselves up to skin the cat, or climb the crosspieces like the rigging of a pirate ship up to the dome-shaped set of bars on top which served as crow's nest. Girls were required to wear dresses to school, and most of us found that our playground activities were seriously hampered by concerns of modesty. Dale and I tried to deal with the restrictions of our clothing by gathering the fullness of our skirts in between our legs and holding the fabric in place with our leg muscles for an improvised trouser effect. Unfortunately it was impossible to climb the monkey bars when doing that.

One day at recess:

"I see London, I see France,

I see Dale's and Jeanne's underpants."

Jet sang out loudly from the bottom of the monkey bars. He was a grinning, crewcut boy in our class whose great purpose in life was to torment Dale and me. He was standing directly below us, neck craned back as far as it would go. With great pudency, we quickly enfolded our skirts into our thighs.

"No, you don't! And besides, just shut up!" I yelled back hotly. My sisters and I were forbidden to use the term "shut up" because our mother deemed it vulgar, but I had no choice but to break that rule when dealing with Jet. He persisted:

"If they're blue or if they're pink,

Man oh man, they sure do stink!"

"They do not! And they're white anyway so you can just shut up right now!" I hissed at him.

Turning to Dale, "Come on, let's go someplace where people aren't so stupid."

We climbed down from the bars and ran over to the Ocean Wave. It was the favorite playground piece of many of the students, being a structure like a huge swinging merry-go-round with room for as many as twenty children to ride at once. Facing inward and with legs dangling in front of us, we sat on wooden boards joined in the shape of an open hexagon. There were railings to hang onto and the whole structure was suspended by chains from a central pole. A teacher or large student pushed the Ocean Wave like a merry-go-round to start it traveling, and once it picked up speed and the riders began to lean back and forth, the whole contraption rolled up and down in great undulations as it swirled around the pole. Very few, if indeed any, of the children at Plentywood School had ever seen an ocean but many of them felt quite seasick after spending a whole recess riding the Ocean Wave.

Softballs were tossed back and forth on the edges of the playground. The schoolyard lacked enough space for a proper diamond so the game itself was played after school in vacant lots around the town. Our little neighborhood by the county hospital had just enough children for two softball teams of up to six players each. Vinny always served as captain of one team and a boy named Dennis captained the other, and when there were plenty of players they took turns choosing teams made up of both boys and girls. Sometimes fewer players turned out for a game and then my sisters and I might form a team against Dennis and two or three other boys. Vinny and Alex were very strong batters and the girls' team often beat the boys. For each of us, me included although more rarely, there was nothing in the world so satisfying as the sound of the solid smack of your bat's perfect connection with a hard-pitched softball. It was a thing of beauty, the dirty leather ball that had once been white, as it arced over the vacant lot and sailed on toward the golf course.

With smaller teams of only three persons each, the usual rules had to be changed. The team at bat provided a rotating catcher so that the team in the field could have one outfielder on each side of the pitcher. It was not necessary to tag a base runner to put that person out; rather, the runner must be crossed by the ball. Whoever fielded the softball after a hit then took aim and rolled it like a long-range bowling ball directly across the path of the runner, and in front of the next base. If the fielder skillfully judged the runner's speed and rolled the ball force-fully and accurately, it was an easy out; but if a runner moved very quickly, she or he could leap right over the rolling ball and then make it all the way around to home plate while the ball was being retrieved. The softball games became highly competitive marathons of play. No one wanted to go home the loser, so the games just continued on and on until it was much too dark to see clearly or until someone's mother hollered out her kitchen door that supper was ready.

OUTDOOR GAMES WERE POSTPONED one springtime when torrential rains fell for several weeks in a row, a very rare occurrence in that part of the Great Plains. Huge puddles flooded the potholes of dirt roads all over town, and as the inundation continued puddles connected onto other puddles to make a canal system through the roads. Wherever the soil was soft or not protected by a covering of early grass more puddles formed. As the hard rain beat into and bounced up from all the little ponds and pools, children stranded indoors watched the bubbling witches' brew through their windows and wondered if the downpour would ever end.

It did at last. Town residents awakened one morning to see steam rising from the sodden roads and fields, and to feel the dense humid-ity of the tropics in our northern Montana locale.

A few days later, little life forms churned up in each body of water. Wiggling specks of protoplasm grew into ovoidal swimming larvae, and these squirmed into round head-bodies with flat whisking tails. The waters seethed with an epidemic of tadpoles, to the great delight of the town's children. The jittery little creatures so completely filled each pool, puddle, and pond that now it seemed like the imagined witches' brew had thickened into a simmering stew.

Monitoring the tadpoles' evolution was a fascinating science les-son to Vinny, Alex, and me. There were especially large puddles in the open field next to our house, and thousands of specimens were there for us to study. One afternoon we saw through our living room windows that several neighborhood boys had gathered out in the field and were bobbing animatedly between the puddles.

"What are those boys doing out there?" Vinny wondered. She went to get her black rubber boots from the hall. "Come on, guysie-wisies," she said, "let's go see what they're up to."

Alex and I pulled on our own boots—a pretty shade of red rather than dull black like Vinny's—and followed our older sister. The three of us slushed through the thick mud of our yard and out into the field. Clyde, a boy whose family had recently moved into the newly built house across the street from ours, was entertaining the other boys with his antics.

"Hey, Clyde," Vinny called out, "what are you guys doing?"

"Experiments," Clyde yelled back. "We're doing science experiments. Come here and I'll show you."

I smiled as my boots squished through the mud. I really admired Clyde. He was two years older than I and such a smart boy. He was always mixing things together with his chemistry set to burn holes through various surfaces, and he had blasted homemade tin can rockets higher than his family's two-story house. He was tall for his age and wore black leather motorcycle-style boots in all kinds of weather with his blue jeans tucked into the tops. Clyde was the only person I had ever met who did not eat sweets. Instead, he saved and hoarded all the candy that he had collected at Halloween and received in his Christmas stocking and Easter basket, and then he sold these goodies to the neighborhood children, taking for payment their allowances or their marble collections.

As we drew close to Clyde and the boys, he reached into a puddle and picked up a fat tadpole. He held it out toward us.

"Here's the experiment," he said and pinched the poor creature's body between his thumb and forefinger. POP! The tadpole exploded.

"You see how loud a noise you can get them to make," Clyde explained as he flicked the remnants of entrails off his fingers and reached again into the water. All around the puddle were little piles and trailings of amphibian guts from Clyde's prior experiments. We were absolutely stunned and my mouth must have dropped open in horror.

"Oh, are you hungry, Junior?" Clyde asked me and he thrust his next victim right into my face, right toward my mouth. As I jerked myself out of range I heard the awful popping sound of the tadpole, then I ran as fast as I could to escape the scene of carnage, dodging the puddles and leaping through the heaps of mud. And after that I really did not admire that boy quite so much.

In just a few days the hordes of spasmodically swimming creatures had reshaped themselves, absorbed their tails, and formed little legs to leap away into the wide world beyond Plentywood.

WHEN I WAS A GIRL, the first of May was a special celebration. During the 1950's, the May Day festivities were clearly not meant to honor the workers of the world, despite our town's Communist history. Nor were the festivities an apparent welcome to Spring because often we were struck by late snowfalls and wintry winds well into the month. The gaiety of May Day arose from the town's abiding belief that the seasons probably would change and the soil probably would be thawed enough to plant. We celebrated the likelihood of Spring.

The custom on May Day was to surprise friends and relatives with little decorated baskets filled with candy, peanuts, and flowers, if any had appeared. If there were only dandelions blooming after a cold spring, then children gathered those and looped their sticky stems together to attach to a basket's handle. In the years when lilacs were already beginning to open their sweet buds, small clusters were cut and tucked into the May baskets. The lovely fragrance rubbed off onto the fingers of those preparing the gifts and rewarded their labors.

Many people bought pleated crepe paper May baskets in pastel colors from the Ben Franklin five-and-dime store on Main Street, but my sisters and I, instructed by our mother, liked to make our own baskets out of bright sheets of construction paper. One style we made by weaving strips of contrasting papers, then folding the flat weaving into a square basket shape, stapling the corners, and attaching a handle.

Another May Day container, good for holding a large amount of treats, was a simple cone rolled from a sheet of the colored paper, with a wide handle added. That was the style Alex always made for Gramp because it could hold a lot of salted-in-the-shell peanuts underneath the candy. We attached a little tag onto each basket, with the name of the friend for whom it was intended, then filled the baskets with jelly beans, butterscotch disks in cellophane, and corn candy. Flowers were the final touch, and the baskets were ready for delivery.

My sisters and I each filled a shoe box with our gifts and headed out to make deliveries. The little baskets were given away with great secrecy. A girl went to the front door of her friend's house and carefully set the basket in a place where it could be noticed before being stepped upon. Then, having already surveyed the yard for a suitable place to hide, she rang the doorbell and dashed off to conceal herself behind a bush or fence. After giving away all her baskets, she would return home to find several that had been left for her. Most boys did not choose to celebrate May Day.

ONE SPRINGTIME an exciting new enterprise opened in a vacant office space, the one left empty when the town's oldest attorney-at-law, eighty-five-year-old Ludwig Gustafson finally decided to retire. The new venture was announced in bright pink paint on a wide piece of muslin stretched across the building's window facing Main Street:

MISS DOTTIE'S SCHOOL OF DANCE

Mother decided that her three older daughters must take advantage of this rare artistic opportunity, and she signed us up for tap dance classes. My best friend Dale and I attended the class for the youngest students.

Miss Dottie was an extremely plump, extremely perky woman with a mane of dark curly hair which she tossed expressively when she talked, and which of its own accord bounced frenetically when she tapped. Her rounded cheeks were deeply pierced by dimples and her broad smile was more than infectious; it provoked pleasureful laughter.

On the first day of class Miss Dottie measured her students' feet so she could order their tap shoes from a store in Missoula. In the meantime the girls wore their school shoes to dance in, and we all tried to stomp hard enough to imitate the rich clattering sounds made by our teacher's metal taps. Miss Dottie's shoes were two-toned, black and white, and had high heels. When she demonstrated a step for the class, dancing alone, the clearly beating rhythms of her taps upon the wooden floor sounded like the trotting of a perfectly trained parade horse, perhaps an elegant Arabian. Then, however, when the rows of girls joined Miss Dottie to try the step, her perfect hoof beats dissolved into our cacophonous pounding, which was more like a herd of stampeding mustangs.

After a couple of weeks, all of the students' tap shoes were delivered to Miss Dottie's school. They were the most beautiful shoes I had ever seen: black patent leather with black grosgrain ribbon ties, those long enough to create a fat bow across the instep. Now the students began to sound much better as we traveled with a step/heel, step/heel, heel/step, heel/step, double-ball-change across the floor. Miss Dottie was a wonderful teacher and the girls in her classes made rapid progress. She decided that her dance school must present a recital.

Miss Dottie began teaching a special dance to each of her classes, using a theme for each group, with music and costumes to match. The class of high school girls began working on some fast-rhythmed songs by the Andrews Sisters. Vinny's class was working with a naval theme, dancing to *Anchors Aweigh*, and using some steps from the Scottish hornpipe. Their costumes were short dresses, dark blue with white polka dots, worn with matching bloomers underneath and white sailor hats topside. Alex's class was dancing to a romantic song, *Apple Blossom Time*, set to more of a polka beat than its usual ballad speed, and the girls were to wear crowns of artificial apple blossoms in their hair, and puffy-skirted dresses of bright pink, Miss Dottie's favorite color.

I thought that my group's costume was the best. The sleeveless dress had a short, circular skirt of chartreuse green, the color of light filtering through a jungle canopy, chosen because our song was about the jungle. It was a popular piece played on the radio, called *Bongo, Bongo, Bongo.* It moved to a slower beat than the music chosen for the older girls and the accentuated cadence of the song was easy to tap to:

Bon-go, Bon-go, Bon-go
I don't want to leave the Con-go
NO! NO! NO!
Bin-gle, Ban-gle, Bun-gle
I'm so hap-py in the Jun-gle
I RE-FUSE TO GO!

After several weeks of practice, the recital was held in the school auditorium. The performance became the social event of the season as hordes of friends, relatives, and neighbors of the dancers crowded into the school. Eager spectators filled the seats on the main floor of the auditorium and the overflow crowd sat in the old wooden balconies along the s des of the room.

The opening number was *Bongo, Bongo, Bongo.* Dale and I were the two leaders each of us with a line of girls behind her, and we slowly, carefully tapped our way onto the stage from opposite sides. Stomp/kick, stomp/kick, stomp/kick came the mostly together rattling beats of twenty-four little black patent leather tap shoes. When Dale and I met in the middle of the stage we turned our lines to face the audience and perform our dance. Shuffle/step/ball-change, reverse, shuffle/step/ball-change....we were right on the beat. Then, with the phrase, *NO! NO! NO!* we all flexed our skinny arms like muscle men, and the audience burst into delighted laughter. The song continued, we twirled, and the amusement of the crowd settled down, but only temporarily. On the emphatic last few words of each stanza the choreography called for flexing our arm muscles, and whenever we did that, the audience couldn't refrain from laughing at us.

Some of the little girls on stage began to think that the strong man gestures were pretty funny too, and soon many in our group were laughing along with the audience. Some of the tappers were so overcome with giggles that they forgot to keep their feet tapping, and the dance ended somewhat in chaos. Dale and I, as the leaders, responsibly kept ourselves from laughing too hard, and we were able to finish the final arm-flexing at the end of our music. The room erupted into applause. We would be a hard act to follow. As I curtsied to the audience from the stage, I could see my parents and grandparents clapping enthusiastically in the front row of the large auditorium, and I felt such a flush of pride that I decided right then to become a dancer when I grew up.

Miss Dottie had talked about the *Fabulous Nicholas Brothers* who tap-danced together in the movies, and I decided that I, Alex, and Vinny could become the *Fabulous Janson Sisters*, tap-dancing our way to fame and glory.

My plans came to an abrupt end, however, when two days after the recital Miss Dottie moved her dance school to Fargo, North Dakota, for financial reasons. The School of Dance had been like a tumbleweed in a sense; it had rolled briskly into town, stayed oh-so-briefly, then lifted up and rolled away across the broad prairie.

WHEN THE MUDDY EARTH had thoroughly dried out on the golf course hills, eager members of the club returned to play. Because of the irregularities and obstacles on the course, golfers were always losing and leaving behind golf balls and colored tees, and these, my sisters and I figured, were fair game for scavengers. So one afternoon as a few popcorn clouds floated across the bright sky, Vinny, Alex, and I set off to hike on those hills and see what treasures we could find. As I slammed the door behind us, a Cadillac pulled up to the curb in front of our house.

"Hi, Louetta," we called as we crossed the yard.

"Oh, Lavinia, Alexandra, little Jeanne! You girls get bigger and prettier each time I see you," a melodious voice sang out from the car window.

Louetta, the egg lady, lived on her chicken farm east of Plentywood near the town of Westby. She was chic. She wore her dark hair pulled back in an elegant French roll and she drove a huge pink Cadillac to deliver her eggs. On her once-a-fortnight delivery day she would fill up the trunk of the Caddy with her eggs laid out in molded cardboard trays, each one carrying two-and-a-half-dozen eggs, and layers of the trays were delicately balanced in corrugated cardboard boxes. Louetta had a route of regular customers in town and she loved to stop and gossip with each one as she brought the order of eggs up to the door. She was especially friendly with our mother and she always came inside to perch on a stool at the kitchen counter and drink coffee and nibble Mother's homebaked cookies. Our mother found a conversation with Louetta to be a refreshing break from the banality of household chores and the constant company of young children.

Like our mother, Louetta had travelled extensively when she was younger. She had visited many of the famous cities of Europe, and had even lived in some, and there was a great deal of speculation among her customers about why such a vital and worldly woman had ended up delivering eggs to the small towns of northeastern Montana. It was clear that she did not really need the money generated by the egg business, evidence of that being rather obvious in the form of her luxurious delivery vehicle. Furthermore, her clothing apparently did not come from the J.C. Penney store on Main Street. She wore elegantly tailored sheath-and-jacket suits, made of pink- or peach-colored doupioni, with matching high heels. On her more casual days Louetta wore slim black Capri pants with a white silk blouse and a red chiffon scarf neatly knotted at her throat.

"Come in, Louetta, it's so nice to see you." Our mother always greeted Louetta with an undisguised eagerness for their friendly exchange. "Let me pour you a cup of coffee."

"Thank you, darling," Louetta chirped in return. She sipped lightly at her coffee as Lorraine placed her eggs in the refrigerator, then their conversing continued:

"Have you noticed those new houses they're putting up on the hillside just below the cemetery?" Lorraine asked.

"No," said Louetta. "Well, close to the cemetery, you say? That's indecent. The whole hill should be left alone to keep the peace and quiet of those resting up there."

"They could build closer to the golf course or out there in that field next to us. Then that blasted wind wouldn't push so hard against our windows." Lorraine shook her head and let out a sigh.

"Well, Lorraine darling, maybe Plentywood isn't exactly paradise on earth, but I think that wherever you live you can make it the center of the universe." Louetta beamed fondly at her friend.

Lorraine's lips turned up slightly in a wistful smile and she nodded as if she wished she could believe that. She had been born in the territory of Hawaii and had lived in many exotic and beautiful places before she married Oscar. A small, isolated town on the northern Great Plains was far, far, from her idea of the center of the universe. The two women drank their coffee and looked out the dining room picture window at the prairie grass set to shimmering by waves of wind.

Meanwhile, Vinny, Alex, and I circled the golf course looking for lost treasures while carefully avoiding the pair of club members who were golfing that afternoon. The far north side of the nine-hole course was a favorite destination of ours, a place we called a chalk butte, where a tall hill had been cut away on one side by time and the elements to create an irregularly stair-stepped limestone cliff. We had frequently practiced our mountain climbing skills on that bluff, and we had also found many natural treasures there in the sedimentary rock formations. Once we had discovered the fossil of a tiny shell, and Dad said it was evidence that millions of years ago an ancient ocean had covered our familiar sea of prairie. Over many visits to that cliff we had collected agates, pink quartz crystals, and pieces of isinglass that split apart into transparent flakes.

"I'll beat you to the top," challenged Vinny. She tied the arms of her canvas jacket around her waist. "Okay. Get set, go!"

She began to climb the rough side of the butte. Alex hustled to try to overtake Vinny but I, who had no chance of beating either of them, took my time. When I finally reached the last length of the limestone face and struggled to pull myself to the top, Alex stretched her arm over the edge and offered a steadying hand to help drag me up. Alex could be sweeter than grape jelly on a marshmallow when she chose.

The three of us stood at the edge of the cliff for a moment catching our breath and looking over the hills toward Canada. Dad said that you could actually see into Canada, a whole separate country, from the height of the golf course hills, but I never could see a difference among all the fields stretching out before me. Turning to the west, we noticed that the color of the sky had changed dramatically during our climb. It was now inked over into an intense shade of blackish blue. The puffy white clouds had disappeared; perhaps they had billowed together to form the threatening column approaching us. It was an ugly gun-metal-gray color. It came up fast and hovered giantly above our bluff. There was a sudden boom of thunder that seemed to shake the ground we stood upon, then tiny hailstones burst from the immense cloud and pattered down around us. They were not even half the size of the teenies in my marble collection, but we knew that that could change quickly.

"We had better get home fast," Alex said soberly. The three of us began to run down the grassy-sloped side of the big hill. When we reached the bottom, the hailstones had grown to the size of regular marbles, and they stung coldly as they struck against our skin.

"Hold your jacket over your head and run like the dickens!" yelled Vinny. When I heard Vinny say "dickens" I knew we were in trouble. There was no place to stop for shelter on the bare hills of the golf course so we stretched our jackets taut and held them above us to deflect the hailstones as we raced for home. The hail pelted down mercilessly, the hard balls bouncing off the ground as if they were made of rubber, not ice. We ran awkwardly, hunched over and faces turned toward the ground, but at last we reached the road near our house. Gasping, we raced the final stretch. We felt on our arms and kicked with our feet hailstones that were almost the size of golf balls.

Mother had been watching for us at the front door and she quickly opened it as we ran up the sidewalk. We stumbled into the house and sank to our knees on the floor, soaked and bruised and out of breath. Mother and Louetta brought towels and patted our wet skin and hair as we sat still, stunned by the downpour of hail we had just run through. We could see through the living room windows that the hailstones were now as huge as softballs. They looked like they were being thrown fast and furiously by a celestial pitcher gone berserk. They pounded the roof.

"Oh no!" exclaimed Louetta slapping her chin. "Look at that! I forgot to close my trunk!" In her eagerness to visit our mother she had hurried into the house and left the trunk of the pink Cadillac wide open. It seemed that the force of the hail might push it closed for her.

As we watched the heavy hail and listened to its reverberant drumming, it seemed like it would never end. But the more cataclysmal events of weather often stop as suddenly as they start, and this hailstorm followed that pattern. The abrupt silence after the hail ended was quickly tempered by the rhythmic dripping of streams of water from the icy globs dissolving on the roof.

We went outside to a world completely transformed. The darkness was cut through with beams of light and a spectacular shining rainbow was stretched across the sky above the golf course hills. The freshly washed sun lit up the beads of moisture on the grass so they sparkled like millions of jewels.

When we looked into the open trunk of the Cadillac we saw that all of Louetta's eggs had been smashed by the hailstones. The trunk was a mess. Melting spheres of hail floated in a giant pool of swirled yolks and albumen with shards of shells poking through. Louetta gingerly lifted layer after layer of soaked cardboard trays and looked below. Through the gooey rubble of scrambled shells, eggs, and soggy cardboard she reached down and gently pulled out a single unbroken egg. She held it up high and looked at it in wonder.

"Well, what do you know about that?" Louetta murmured.

COWBOYS AND INDIANS

THE DRAMA OF THE OLD WEST, that historic struggle to tame and exploit the wide open spaces, was the theme of many of the movies that played in the Orpheum Theatre on Main Street in our town. My sisters and I loved those movies and we delighted in the knowledge that our corner of Montana had served as the real life setting for similar western legends. Grandpa Walt knew countless stories about the olden days, several of them heard firsthand when he was a boy, and his connection to that history made it ever vivid in our minds. In addition, the arid land around Plentywood, the hilly prairie sprinkled with sagebrush and dominated by limestone bluffs, resembled those panoramas we saw on the movie screen.

The northeastern section of our state contained some of the last large parcels of acreage available for homesteading in the continental United States during the early years of the 20th century. Waves of farmers and ranchers moved into the area to lay claim to the land. It was a common practice for many of the homesteaders to plant grain crops and also raise cattle or sheep; this diverse usage of the land within the individual owners' spreads prevented the range wars seen in other parts of the West. Another form of strife soon developed, however, with the establishment of large cattle ranches in the wide open spaces of the Big Muddy Creek valley. These ranches opened up opportunities for a number of young men to find employment as cowboys, and for others to work as rustlers.

Many of those who became bandits started out as honest cowhands. Some deserted their ranch duties and switched to a life of thievery after becoming discontented with the low pay and long hours of hard work on the range. Others became outlaws while still in the employ of crooked ranch barons, men who coerced their naive young cowhands into stealing cattle or horses from rival ranchers. For men who wanted to make a bundle of money quickly, and who had no scruples about how to do so, the livestock rustling business, and particularly that involving horses, was booming in northeastern Montana. The area that was later to become Sheridan County was a part of the vast Valley County in those days, 14,000 square miles of fenceless prairie range wide open with possibilities for lawlessness. The Valley County seat in Glasgow was separated from the new settlement of Plentywood by well over a hundred miles as the crow might fly across the Big Muddy Creek and the Ft. Peck Indian Reservation. From his headquarters in Glasgow, the Chief Stock Inspector attempted to regulate and police the flourishing livestock industry, and for this he enlisted the help of Canadian Mounties based in Regina. With a tinge of misplaced pride, the Inspector warned the Mounties that Valley County was the "most lawless and crooked county in the Union, and the Big Muddy was the worst part of it."

Part of the problem came from the lack of regulation in the ranching business. Each rancher could register as many brands as he wanted, and this led to confusion and fraud in identifying ownership of the stock. In addition, placement of the brand on an animal was not standardized so a single animal might be branded in several places with the marks of competing ranchers. Many ranchers simply chose not to use brands at all, and if their livestock were hijacked on the range and quickly branded they could not be recovered.

The influx of homesteaders into the area created a demand for good horses to plow the newly unsodded fields, and a black market thrived in the trade of stolen animals. A horse valued at $10 when sold honestly could be resold by a thief for $200 to a needful emigrant farmer. Cattle were slightly less profitable on the black market, but they still fetched a good price and sometimes entire herds were brazenly seized and resold over in North Dakota or across the border in Canada.

The rustlers' exploits were still being talked about when Gramp was a young boy in Valley County. In recounting the legendary crimes, people spoke of two varieties of Big Muddy outlaw. There was the harsh-speaking, gun-brandishing, vulgar sort, and naturally, these men had caused fear throughout the land. Other outlaws, however, had totally shunned violence and were so well-mannered that they inspired admiration and a desire to emulate their deeds. The most famous of the rustlers were Left-handed Jones, Red Nelson, Tommy Ryan, the Pigeon-toed Kid, and Dutch Henry Ieuch (not to be confused with a similarly named outlaw of Colorado, and another who operated in Utah). Left-handed Jones and Red Nelson were co-leaders of the largest and most disreputable of the gangs, one that boasted thirty desperadoes. Both men had committed numerous crimes under various aliases before ending up in the Big Muddy area, and both were rumored to be utterly ruthless. Between them, Red must have been the better marksman because he was known to be one of the few actual murderers among the outlaws of Valley County.

Tommy Ryan was tall and supremely handsome with deep blue eyes. His demeanor was refined and gentlemanly, and he always wore a blue silk cravat that perfectly matched his eyes. Tommy's charm and appearance were such that female bank customers being robbed by him felt no fear, but swooned anyway. Later, when they recounted details of the crime to their friends, these women were greatly envied. Ryan was an adamantly peaceful man by nature but he did carry two revolvers to assure success in his chosen line of work. He couldn't very well empty the vault of the Reserve Bank by brandishing just his blue cravat.

The Pigeon-toed Kid, so-named for his ambulatory lack of grace, was a latecomer in Valley County, having begun his thieving career in Canada. He arrived in the area after accomplishing an amazing escape from the Mounties, showing great physical prowess despite his moniker by leaping out of a train window. He made his way across the border and sought work on a ranch, where the owner soon recruited him to steal horses from other ranchers. Pigeon-toe decided it would be more profitable to drop the middle man, the greedy ranch owner, and to work free-lance, and he did this so successfully, despite his notable clumsiness, that he was soon one of the most wanted men in the county.

But the most sought-after and the most celebrated of the Big Muddy outlaws was Dutch Henry Ieuch, a short and stocky man with gold teeth gleaming beneath a small mustache. The rustler spoke with a heavy German accent and practiced courtly manners that rivaled Tommy Ryan's. All who encountered him testified to the prepossessing charm of the man, and he was famous for his humor and storytelling skills. Many tales were circulated about the helpful deeds he performed for homesteaders and small-time ranchers, as well as his pecuniary generosity to them. Dutch gave away most of the money he stole and some folks began calling him the "Robin Hood of Valley County." In common with Tommy Ryan, Dutch Henry firmly believed in nonviolence and this he practiced throughout his career.

At the turn of the century Culbertson, Montana, was known as the roughest and toughest of the cattle towns. It was virtually run by competing gangs of rustlers. Thirteen saloons were located along its Main Street, and that was more than twice the number of small stores and feed supply operations in the town. Gunshots were heard frequently in the saloons, nighttime and day, and in the livery stables more shots testified to a form of leisure time recreation there, the target practice challenges of off-duty cowboys.

The lawlessness of the town and surrounding countryside created an unsolved mystery in my family history. It happened a few years before my grandfather and his parents and brothers arrived in that part of the country. An uncle of Walter's had already emigrated from Minnesota with his family and filed his homestead claim a safe distance northeast of Culbertson, that hotbed of un-Lutheran debauchery, in the plain countryside near Dagmar.

On a bright day in early spring, the family sent its oldest son, Walter's cousin Frank who was around thirteen years of age, to pick up a supply of flax seed and other necessities from a feed store in Culbertson. Frank hitched up the family's single horse to the farm wagon, swung himself up onto the board seat, and with a hearty "Haw" from his almost masculine voice, he turned out of the claim and onto the wagon tracks that led toward glittering Medicine Lake in the distance, and the thirty miles beyond to Culbertson.

Along the way, he may have heard birds warbling their springtime joy. He may have noticed light green prairie grasses newly burst from the earth. Perhaps cottony streamers of cloud caught his eye and inspired a young man's daydreams as he idly held the reins of his father's horse and traveled that familiar passage to the town. Of those things we do not know. The boy, the horse, and the wagon were never seen again.

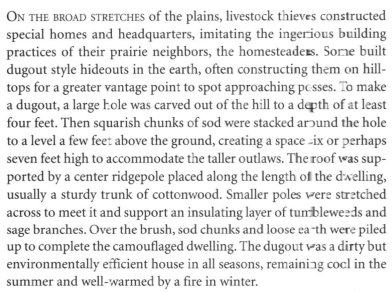

ON THE BROAD STRETCHES of the plains, livestock thieves constructed special homes and headquarters, imitating the ingenious building practices of their prairie neighbors, the homesteaders. Some built dugout style hideouts in the earth, often constructing them on hilltops for a greater vantage point to spot approaching posses. To make a dugout, a large hole was carved out of the hill to a depth of at least four feet. Then squarish chunks of sod were stacked around the hole to a level a few feet above the ground, creating a space six or perhaps seven feet high to accommodate the taller outlaws. The roof was supported by a center ridgepole placed along the length of the dwelling, usually a sturdy trunk of cottonwood. Smaller poles were stretched across to meet it and support an insulating layer of tumbleweeds and sage branches. Over the brush, sod chunks and loose earth were piled up to complete the camouflaged dwelling. The dugout was a dirty but environmentally efficient house in all seasons, remaining cool in the summer and well-warmed by a fire in winter.

Other hideouts were made of willow stalks, so naturally these dwellings were built near the streams where willows grew—Wolf Creek, the Poplar River, and sections of Big Muddy Creek. This particular shelter was intended for the temperate times of the year; it was not suited to withstand the harsh winds and frigid lows of the winter. Large mats were woven by a simple crisscross overlapping of the willow canes, and these mats were supported by a few poles and lashed together to make the hut. The willow hideouts were concealed in riparian foliage and they blended seamlessly into the landscape.

The well-known Outlaw Trail cut through Valley County. It was an escape route of hideouts and safe houses that had been organized by Butch Cassidy. He and his gang were wide-ranging robbers, and his series of refuge points stretched all the way from Mexico to Canada. The final northern stops on the Trail were along Big Muddy Creek and in the badlands, and one of these hideouts was directly north of Plentywood. It consisted of two large caves, one for the robbers and rustlers, and one for their mounts. When Butch permanently abandoned his hideouts on the Outlaw Trail to pursue other opportunities in Bolivia, the outlaws and rustlers of Valley County took over his caves.

By the time Walter and his family arrived in Valley County during the homestead rush, only a few of the Big Muddy bandits were still terrorizing the area. Many of the outlaws remained nearby but they realized that a county swarming with emigrants would soon be swarming with lawmen. Some of the badmen retired from their profession, and others stayed entrenched in their hideouts, emerging only occasionally for minor jobs of thievery. The killer Red Nelson was one who had noticed that times were changing and he decided he should go straight. He turned himself in. He was held in the county jail in Glasgow and tried for murder and rustling, but he was soon released due to insufficient evidence. Several of the other livestock thieves had been arrested and put on trial at some time during their careers, but not one was ever convicted by a court. There was just not enough hard evidence or eyewitness testimony to prove their crimes.

The handsome and well-beloved bandit Tommy Ryan also tried to become an honest man. He felt attached to the land where he had spent his thieving career and he consulted a lawyer about how he might obtain amnesty from the states of Montana and North Dakota so he could continue to live on the northern plains. When he was told his Montana amnesty would include extradition to North Dakota and there a probable ninety-nine years in jail for armed bank robbery, Tommy discarded his hopes for upright citizenship and went permanently on the lam.

Although most of the outlaws of the Big Muddy were gun-toters who fired their weapons frequently, few of them ever managed to wound, much less kill, the lawmen and posse members who pursued them. Most of the famous bandits, however, ended up being dispatched violently by an armed official or a disgruntled comrade-in-arms. The first to go was the ruthless Left-handed Jones, killed by a deputy while he was peaceably eating a pancake breakfast on a ranch near Scobey. Afterwards, people thought that Left-handed should have been allowed a chance to go for his gun, and many mourners packed the church for his funeral.

A couple of years later, across the border in North Dakota, Dutch Henry was robbed and murdered on an isolated road by a young man who had once idolized him. Dutch's adoring public had a hard time accepting the dismal circumstances of his death; people would have preferred a blaze of glory for his departure. The whole area mourned Dutch deeply, and newspapers reported on his career's particulars, actual and otherwise, for several months.

The physically inept Pigeon-toed Kid, who had vowed never to be taken alive, was tracked by a Deputy to a shack outside of Poplar. The lawman demanded that the Kid surrender, and he refused. Thereupon the Deputy charged into the building and in the ensuing gunfight, Pigeon's less than skillful handling of his firearm allowed him to keep the vow that he'd made.

After he failed in his attempt to go straight, the charming Tommy Ryan, like Butch Cassidy before him, headed to South America to re-vitalize his career. In Argentina he and his comrades, like Butch and Sundance, were gunned down by soldiers. These notorious deaths made headlines when our Grandpa Walt was just learning to read and they made quite an impression on the lad.

A LONG-RUNNING DROUGHT brought hard times to his family's home-stead, and so twelve-year-old Walter went to work on a cattle ranch near Comertown, almost twenty miles from his parents' spread. He started out doing general chores and driving a team and wagon on errands for the rancher. The errands required some travel in those days, with the main suppliers still located near the train station at Culbertson. Young Walter had to drive sixty miles to pick up the rancher's goods, then back at a slower pace with a full wagon. The railroad town had settled down a little with the taming of the outlaw gangs, and there were no longer thirteen saloons along Main Street. The surrounding area still teemed with off-duty cowboys and pos-sible rustlers, though, and Walter remembered well how his cousin Frank had disappeared from the face of the earth on his way to

Culbertson. Our grandfather said that the rancher gave him a pistol to carry on those trips but it always remained hidden under the seat of the wagon. He didn't want to fire it and he never had to.

One time Walter was caught in a violent rainstorm as he drove to Culbertson to pick up a load. The wind blew ferociously and the rain beat down so hard that it spooked the horses and the boy could barely control them. He had to take refuge at a ranch near Antelope which was owned by a man he barely knew. The bachelor rancher welcomed young Walter and helped him to put up the team in the barn, then led him into the single-roomed shack to spend the night. There were four grown men already in the little house and they were what Walter's mother would have called "rowdies." They were playing cards for money, cussing, and drinking whiskey, very sinful activities in the eyes of the quiet Swedish boy.

But more shocking still were the sleeping arrangements. Walter was shown to the bunk he would have to share with a man he was told had consumption and who lifted his hand in greeting as he coughed raggedly into a dirty handkerchief. To a twelve-year-old boy, and especially the son of a nurse, "consumption" was a frightening word and although he climbed up into the bunk with the gasping and gagging man, Walter did not sleep a wink that night. At the first glimmer of daybreak he sneaked out of the shack, harnessed up the horses, and drove away without any breakfast to the train stop another forty miles in the distance.

By the time he was fourteen Walter had become a cowboy, and after a couple of years he was hired on by a larger ranch near Poplar. The smooth brown leather chaps he had worn in his cowboy days were still hanging in a metal cabinet in Gramp's basement. Grandma Christina called that repository her *Fibber McGee* closet because she said it was full of old junky things that should be thrown out. She never threw out the chaps, though, because she remembered how handsome the teen-aged Walter had been when he wore them.

Christina had been a pretty, but no-nonsense schoolteacher tending her charges in a little country school when she first saw the young man who would become her husband. Students and teacher were outside the small wooden building having their lunchtime when the young cowhand rode up. He stopped to draw some water at the well and then he shyly spoke a few friendly words to the schoolmarm. When he left to rejoin his herd, Christina had watched Walter ride away, staring fixedly until he turned suddenly and waved his hat. She was too embarrassed to wave back, but afterwards she had thought about the young cowboy from time to time. A few years later they met again at the county harvest festival, and shortly thereafter the two were married at the courthouse in Glasgow. So the old chaps had remained as a memento of those bygone days, and we granddaughters liked to touch their smooth surface and sniff their leathery smell.

It was easy for me to picture Gramp as a cowboy, riding his pony across fields of yellow prairie grass and gently moving and calming the cattle by singing to them. In like manner, he often soothed Katie or Johnny to sleep with a soft lullaby. Gramp told us older girls about the nights he had spent on the range many miles from any town. He would listen for the coyotes' lonely howls out in the darkness while he watched golden sparks from the campfire float up to join the stars. After eating supper, which was usually beans, biscuits, and salt pork, young Walter spread out his bedroll beside those of the other boys and men, then laid himself down to count shooting stars before he fell asleep.

"How many did you count in those days, Gramp?" my sisters and I eagerly asked, even though we had heard the story many times.

"Well, I'd usually count none, or maybe one, before I fell asleep," Gramp recalled, his eyes twinkling. "Riding herd was hard work."

The main route for the Poplar ranch's cattle drives crossed the Big Muddy at the town of Homestead, then continued east to North Dakota, joining up with the Soo Line Railroad for shipment. Gramp talked about meeting a painter on one of the cattle drives, a man named Charlie Russell who later became very famous. Charlie was not a hunter but he enjoyed going on hunting trips with his friends so that he could draw the animals. Many antelope herds frequented the area around Medicine Lake, so on a warm day in early autumn the artist and his friends were camping close to the lake.

When the cowboys approached the camp, Charlie immediately noticed the beautiful pony Walter was riding, a pinto named Gypsy, and he asked if he could sketch the young man sitting on his horse. Our grandfather was quite exhausted at the end of a long day of riding the range but he was flattered by the notion of having his portrait and that of the incomparable Gypsy drawn by a "gen-u-ine artist", as his fellows introduced him. So Walter agreed to pose, but he soon fell asleep. He remained in a sound sleep but, skillful cowboy that he was, managed to stay on his horse and only slump a little in the saddle until Charlie had finished the drawing. The artist woke him up and the groggy Walter had a look at the watercolor sketch. His eyes opened wide in amazement. Charlie had carefully captured every detail of the young cowboy's clothing, bedroll, and gear, as well as the distinctive piebald patterns of Gypsy. After that time our grandfather greatly admired Charlie Russell's art and he proudly displayed in a wooden frame the envelope Charlie had decorated with the quick sketch of a wolf along with the message "Thank you Walter and Gypsy."

Charlie drew the image of a wolf because his party had passed through the town of Wolf Point before they set up camp at Medicine Lake. Charlie asked Walter's companions why there were no wolves to be seen anywhere in the vicinity of the town bearing their name, and one of the older cowpokes explained that twenty years before there had been an abundance of wolves in the area but the settlers found them threatening in appearance and habit, so they had taken care of the varmints by killing all that they could find, around a thousand as it turned out. The wolves were long gone, but the memory of their presence had been preserved in the town's name.

THE LIFE OF A COWBOY as Gramp had known it was long gone too, but my sisters and I were sure that it was the best life possible, and our favorite play activity was being cowboys. We knotted up a rope to use for a lasso and we tried twirling it in the air and jumping through it, I with limited success, and we also practiced spinning the loop around and trying to lasso tree branches and bicycle handlebars. We would put on our cowboy hats and tie our neckerchiefs, then practice mounting the huge stationary stallion behind our house, the propane tank. I always needed a boost to climb on, but my sisters could swing up onto the tank like the movie cowboys did. Then all three of us would gallop away on the stallion, fast as the wind across the plains.

Sometimes we pretended that we were pioneers crossing the country in covered wagons. Large cardboard boxes were the wagons headed west, led by Vinny as the wagon master. Alex played a pioneer woman in a long skirt borrowed from our mother, with her dolls sitting up to act as children, and I got to be a young cowboy herding the livestock. Vinny fired her cap gun to start the wagons rolling, just as the trail boss had done in many a movie we had seen. Then, after a long day of traversing the prairie, we scraped out a campfire pit in the dirt, lined it with stones, and set up sticks to form a tripod for the imaginary cooking pot. When Mother brought out jelly sandwiches for our lunch, we roasted them over the pretend coals.

Westerns were the movies most frequently shown at the Orpheum Theatre, and of course they were our favorites. *Shane* had come to town often, and the quiet hero reminded us of Gramp because he did not drink whiskey and he tried to help people peacefully. Shane would resemble our grandfather even more if he had chosen to settle down and become a homesteader rather than riding off into the sunset at the end of the picture. Each time I saw the movie I somehow hoped anew that the ending would change and Shane would stay there on the homestead.

The movies about fighting the Indians were often disturbing to us, and one of the most frightening images was that of a flaming arrow piercing a white canvas wagon cover and bursting into bright Technicolor flames. It was hard to understand why there was so much fighting when there were such amazingly spacious panoramas of land out in the West. Why couldn't the Indians and settlers share it, we wondered. In one movie, *Broken Arrow*, the soldiers and Indians did try to get along together, and the character played by Jimmy Stewart married a beautiful Indian woman in a white buckskin dress. After the wedding, in which the two cut their pointer fingers with a knife and dripped their blood together, peace was short-lived and many misunderstandings led to more fighting and the shocking death of the lovely bride.

Most movies seemed to show the Indians as being wrong in their resistance to the settlement of the West, but my sisters and I found many things to admire about them. We were outdoors girls so we appreciated and envied what we understood to be the Indian way of life—a vitality of being in the open spaces, sleeping in simple tepees beneath the stars, and traveling on beautiful spotted horses. We envied the movie Indian costumes too: the buckskin clothing with long fringes, necklaces with colorful beads and animal teeth, and feathers in lustrous braided hair.

We girls often played that we were Indians. We painted designs on our faces with one of Mother's old lipsticks, and we poked the chicken feathers from Gramp's hens into our braided hair. Sometimes we had elegant pheasant feathers to use also, when Dad had shot one on a hunting trip. We propped up long sticks and lashed them with twine to make the frame for a tepee, then we draped a bed sheet around it for the covering. We scraped out a fire pit, no different from our pioneer one, in the dirt.

Gramp had told us many times how the Plains Indians traveled over the prairies of our area hunting the buffalo long before the Scandinavian settlers came to the place, but we had never seen an Indian on the streets of Plentywood. Dad said that Indians were not allowed to live in our town; they belonged on the Fort Peck Indian Reservation and they were supposed to stay there.

ONE SUMMER DAY, our father took Vinny, Alex, and me on a business trip to Wolf Point, one hundred miles southwest of Plentywood. The highway crossed right through the Fort Peck Indian Reservation, and the three of us were very excited because we would be able to see some real Indians, not the movie Indians, at last. As Dad drove through the reservation, though, we became disappointed because the Chevy was going much too fast for us to clearly see any Indians who may have been in the fields and farmyards that we passed. We kept pestering Dad to tell us when we would get to see the Indians, and then as we drove into Wolf Point, he gestured toward a group of people on the sidewalk. "Look kiddos, there are some real live Indians, there in front of the bar. That's where you look when you want to spot Indians."

The three of us stared. These people did not remotely resemble the proud and beautiful Indians in the movies. These people looked shabby and sad. Some were slumped on a bench and one was lying on the sidewalk. I could barely believe that those people were the Indians, but they must be if Dad said so.

My sisters and I sat in the car while our father took care of his official business in the Wolf Point City Hall. Afterwards, Dad took us to a drive-in for hamburgers and chocolate milkshakes, then we stopped at a gas station to fill up the tank before heading home. Alex and I ran over to use the bathroom and we found that the door to the *Ladies* was locked. We waited for a long time but no one came out, so we went into the station office.

"We can't get into the bathroom," Alex told the man.

"Oh, here's the key," the proprietor said as he handed it over. We had never heard of locking up a gas station bathroom with a key, and we were puzzled

"Why do you keep the door locked?" Alex asked the man as she took the key.

"Well, you know those Indians would start living in there if it wasn't locked," he replied. "They come off the reservation and they're just looking for somewhere to stay here in town while they do their drinking. If I didn't lock that door, honey, it would be 'Home, Sweet Home' for them.'

We went into the bathroom, which was very small and dirty, and then we returned the key to the man. As we drove back to Plentywood I could not stop thinking about how those Indians on the street had looked and then the shocking thing the filling station man had said about Indians. What kind of home would a gas station bathroom be? Would you sleep curled up on that dirty floor? Where would you take a bath? Could people really stand to live that way? Finally I had to ask my father, "Daddy, would an Indian really live in a bathroom?"

Dad glanced back at me and laughed. "You never know," he said. I watched my father's face reflected in the rear-view mirror. He kept on smiling for quite a while but I could not tell if he had been joking. Sometimes it was hard to figure Dad out.

AN INVASION OF PRICKLY PEARS occurred one hot summer on the northern plains, with multitudes of the desert plants bursting through the sod and lying in wait, concealing their sharp spines in the tall prairie grass. For those seeking adventure on the golf course hills, vigilance was required; a long cactus needle could easily puncture the rubber sole of a sneaker. When the clumps of prickly pears eventually produced beautiful waxy blossoms in shades of cream, peach, and lemon yellow, a new kind of treasure was offered up for scavengers.

My friend Dale and I dodged the course's few golfers and combed the hills in search of the semi-concealed flowers. Over several trips, we carefully plucked as many of the stemless blooms as we could carry back to my yard. There we created a spectacular display of the pastel flowers, floating them like water lilies in old coffee cans filled with water, and these we lined up all along the sidewalk. When we ran out of large cans, I filled up the bed of our silver Radio Flyer wagon with the hose, and then we added the rest of the cactus flowers. Dale and I pulled the lovely floating garden over to show the residents of Pioneer Manor, the old folks' home attached to the hospital, leaving a trail of slopping water as we went.

A more common prickly plant that issued forth from the prairie was the tumbleweed, which started out as a smooth-stemmed, jagged-leafed bush, and in its dried-up form became a ball of thorns. The empty fields adjoining our yard were studded with the round, dark-green weeds, and they grew tall and full all summer, providing places between them to hide quickly when we and the other children of the neighborhood played a wide-ranging game of cowboy and Indian hide-and-seek.

The weeds dried up rapidly at the end of the summer, turning from green to golden tan, with the appendages along the branches hardening into points. A swift wind would detach the tumbleweeds from the grip of the earth and send them somersaulting across the prairie, turning quickly over and over, sometimes settling and resting still for a spell, then lifting up and spinning on. Some of the tumbleweeds which rolled across the wide fields were stopped and trapped by the propane tank in our yard, and once Vinny amassed enough of the prickly spheres to pile up and form a jail cell. Then she made Alex and me go inside the mean little structure to test it out. It was a success. Inside, the quarters were as cramped as a dungeon and we could not move around without being tortured by the walls' little thorns.

Our mother thought of a more benign use for the always-present tumbleweeds. One August she began to collect the spiny golden balls as they blew into our yard or rested in the near fields. She was mysteriously silent about her plans for the hoarded weeds, and they remained in a huge pile filling a corner of the basement until after Thanksgiving. Then Mother brought them up the stairs a few at a time, and on our back steps, bundled up against the cold and wearing her calfskin driving gloves for protection, she began to weave the tumbleweeds together with light wire. For several days she continued to connect the tumbleweeds, propping a stepladder over the already attached ones when her work was interrupted. We girls watched her with impatient puzzlement until the form of her creation became apparent: she was making Sheridan County's largest and spikiest Christmas wreath, not out of the traditional but unavailable holly, but from the abundant materials at hand. When she had finished, the oversized wreath stood taller than our one-story house and she climbed carefully up the stepladder to fasten on the appropriate embellishment, a gigantic bow she had fashioned from yards and yards of red fabric.

Mother and Dad rolled the wreath around to the front of the house and Dad anchored it with wire between two box elder trees in our yard. The golden wreath was utterly magnificent against the yard's thick covering of snow, and town residents soon came in crowds to admire it. Unfortunately, the amazing wreath was only briefly on display. Ten days before Christmas, blizzardly winds blasted down from Canada and strewed the tumbleweeds far and wide.

It was more than halfway through the summertime, after the little lake in Gramp's Coulee had dried into a cracked mud bed, but before the busy wheat harvest had begun. Dad and Gramp were working on machines in the quonset, and Vinny, Alex, and I were traipsing down the hill to check on the Coulee's chokecherry crop.

Chokecherries are enigmatic. They seem mysteriously unresolved, like a not-yet-perfected creation from the Garden of Eden, among the flora still in a little test garden when the main operation was irredeemably polluted by sin and closed down.

Chokecherries are paradoxical. They are sweet in appearance, having a shiny, blackish purple color like Bing cherries, but each tiny chokecherry, even when fully ripe, is so sour that a single one can pucker up your entire mouth and part way down your throat, indeed almost making you choke.

Chokecherries are deceptive. They are individually no bigger than a woman's pinkie fingernail, but each one conceals a woody pit only a little smaller than the chokecherry itself. It requires a quick reflex to spit out that pit rather than swallow it as you begin to pucker.

Given these contrary qualities and drawbacks, chokecherries might seem hardly worth the bother of harvesting and sieving. But you would be wrong to disdain them because chokecherries have a lovely, wild and tangy essence like none other. They are truly feral fruits, but well worth the stalking.

Every year when the chokecherries ripened at last, our family picked gallons of the imperfect little cherries and Mother patiently sieved out the seeds and boiled them into a delicious jelly, using plenty of sugar to tame down the tartness.

On this afternoon the chokecherries were still partly reddish in color, far from being ripe, so my sisters and I sat down in the shade of the cottonwoods at the bottom of the Coulee and lazily watched the grasshoppers. Their dusty brown bodies emitted scratchy sounds as they leaped, playing off each other like a discordant strings section of an insect orchestra. Their dull coats so closely matched the gray dirt patches where they landed that they were hard to see between the stalks of dry grass.

Suddenly, the musical trilling of a meadowlark descended upon us, like clear drops of water onto thirsty earth. We sat in silence, hoping for another meadowlark to answer the call of the first, and a series of alternating choruses to follow. But there was no choral reply. The grasshoppers jumped around us.

Then a shadow caught my eye, and above the near hillside I saw the hawk which cast it. It was a huge hawk and it soared incredibly slowly in a wide circle, its dark body pronounced against the cloudless sky. "Look there," I breathed with wonder.

My sisters gazed up at the raptor.

"I have never, ever, seen such a giant hawk," declared Alex.

"Where is she going?" Vinny asked as the hawk's movement arced westward. In long and effortless glides, across the vast spaces she traveled before soaring back to circle again above our hillside. Only the slightest tilting of a wing allowed the magnificent bird to change her direction, and only the briefest up and down flurry of her wings allowed her to soar nearly forever. We were transfixed by the grace and subtlety of her flight.

"If I could be any bird, then I would be a hawk," I said, although I truly loved the meadowlark too. I considered that point. Would I rather soar powerfully, or would I choose to sing beautifully?

This bird circled above us several times, then traced a long ellipse toward the west.

"Look how she keeps coming back toward us," Vinny said.

The hawk had reentered the space above Gramp's Coulee and orbited directly over our heads, high, high above us. We watched her reverently, wondering where she would turn. It was westward again, when she finally changed her course. Vinny leaped up.

"Let's follow her."

Alex and I got to our feet quickly and ran after Vinny through the yellow grass and over the creeping juniper on the slope of the hillside.

The hawk winged strongly in a straight path for a few moments, then she dropped down low and briefly out of sight beyond a bluff. We waited. Our hawk re-ascended suddenly and powerfully.

"Did it catch a mouse or bunny?" I asked Vinny, whose vision was sharp.

"No, she isn't carrying anything," Vinny replied thoughtfully. "I really wonder what that hawk is trying to do."

"I think she is leading us somewhere," said Alex.

Curious and delighted, we watched that mysterious hawk, our necks craning upward, and we followed her for a good distance, stepping around granite stones and through the tall grasses. At last we climbed over a gentle ridge, and saw that our hawk had stopped traveling and was again tracing a single, wide circle in the deep blue sky. So gracefully, so very slowly did she glide that her continuing flight seemed impossible. What kind of force held her high when her wings stopped moving? As I pondered that mystery, I felt my gaze being pulled down from the sky and into the little coulee below the ridge. It had gently sloping sides like Gramp's Coulee, and on the flat, grassy bottom I saw a perfect circle about twelve feet in diameter made up of large stones spaced evenly apart.

I knew exactly what that circle was, and I was so astonished to see it that all I could gasp out was "Oh my ...". I pointed down at the circle and began running toward it. My sisters gasped too, and ran with me. We had heard many times about such a circle but we had never before seen one.

"An Indian ring!" Vinny shouted. "A real-live Indian ring!"

"Hooray!" Alex and I screamed.

Gramp had told us about finding Indian rings in the countryside when he was a boy. An Indian ring was the circle of rocks which had held down the edges of a buffalo skin tepee so it could not be blown over by the steady prairie wind. Gramp had explained that when the Indian people packed up to move to another camp they took down and carried away the wooden poles and the sewn skins that covered the tepees, but of course they had not taken along the heavy stones. Those were left in place to be used another time. As young boys, Walter and his brothers Emanuel and Rasmus had believed that seeing an Indian ring would bring good luck. They had combed the fields and valleys in search of those forgotten rings, and they had found them occasionally in those olden days. We never imagined that we could find one.

We ran at full speed down the slope of the coulee, then right into the middle of the circle. Alex and I started dancing and spinning with our arms outstretched, twirling faster and faster. Virny walked slowly around the circle, reverently studying and touching each stone. Then I remembered our hawk and I looked up from the circle. The sky was empty.

Later we told Gramp all about the Indian ring and how the large hawk had seemed to lead us right to it, and he nodded his head. "Sure, they say that hawks were always special to the Indian people."

As we drove along the blacktop back to town, Alex started singing *Home, Home on the Range* and everyone joined in. It was one of our favorite songs.

Oh give me a home where the buffalo roam
Where the deer and the antelope play....

We all knew it was not possible to see a buffalo roam any more, but we frequently saw both antelope and deer in the countryside. And even beautiful red foxes were sighted sporadically, especially near the town of Redstone for some reason. Perhaps the foxes thought they could blend into the sandstone surroundings closely enough to escape the fate of their ancient cousins who had lived in the area around Wolf Point.

Next, Dad started singing *Oh Susannah*, and then we sang *Skip to My Lou* on and on until no more verses could be thought of or made up. All the other favorite songs followed, folk songs that were sung in music class at school, and these always evoked thoughts of the Old West, of the pioneers and cowboys: *Whoopee-ti-yi-yo—Get along Little Dogies, Old Dan Tucker, Polly Wolly Doodle, Goodby Old Faint—I'm A' Leavin' Cheyenne, Sweet Betsy from Pike, My Darlin' Clementine, Buffalo Gals,* and a special state song, *My Home's in Montana.* I loved that

song because it described the life of a cowboy, the life that Gramp had
known when he was young.

> *My home's in Montana, I wear a bandana,*
> *My spurs are of silver, my pony is gray,*
> *When riding the ranges, my luck never changes,*
> *With foot in my stirrup, I gallop away.*
>
> *When far from the ranches, I chop the pine branches*
> *To heap on the campfire when daylight grows pale,*
> *When I have partaken, of beans and of bacon*
> *I whistle a merry old song of the trail.*

STORMS

RAIN IN THE ARID LAND AROUND PLENTYWOOD was preceded by a deliciously fresh smell in the air, the fragrance of salvation to the farmers. Long before others noticed it, Gramp and his friends could sniff an impending rainfall and declare, "Yup, smells like rain," and rarely were they mistaken. The rain fell gently at first, and on the unpaved streets of our town the wet spatters sent up little clouds of dust as they hit. Then, as the drops soaked into bare ground, they spread dotted patterns of damp all across the dryness. Outside of town, after a good rain fell onto farmers' gray fields, the moisture brought forth an earthen aroma of such vitality that a stranger might believe the illusion of a fertile topsoil in those parts.

A thunderstorm over the prairie was a thing of great beauty and sometimes great violence. Many a storm began with the theatrical appearance of a giant anvil cloud glowing with hues of dawn and dusk in its towering form. Like a charismatic actor, the cloud commanded all attention as he strutted slowly across his stage. Part of the show was the costuming; while he postured, the great cloud added layers and shadows to his raiment. At last, when all was ready, the lights darkened and a booming thunderclap signaled that the tempest had begun.

At other times, a storm might come roaring out of nowhere in a quicksilver fury. When the crashes of thunder came suddenly, and were close to deafening, one could imagine Thor above wielding his hammer, smashing colossal granite boulders into smaller pieces that he could hurl into the farmers' fields. Thus he might combine in a vindictive manner his two occupations as Norse god of thunder and agriculture.

Lightning appeared in different forms during the storms, but always evoked the sense of a magical happening. The thunderbolt variety stretched down from sky to earth in sharp zigzags and resembled the cryptic writing of a conjurer, the secret symbols he was flashing across the gloomy heavens. Other lightning was diffused among overlaying clouds, spreading and glowing with a greenish light, like the wide curtains hung around a witch's lair, eerily illuminated by her fire within.

Many summer storms were empty show, all sound and fury but carrying no precipitation. The dry cloud masses emitted a smell of pent-up dustiness and a stifling feeling very unlike the fresh aroma carried by rainclouds.

When a storm was very far away, a miniature version of its drama could be seen but not heard across the vast space of the grassland. The distant storm was strangely unreal and unthreatening in its silence, with the lightning blurring dreamily into a yellow-rose stripe in the strata of dark clouds. The light seemed like the doorway to a whole other world that had briefly come to life, and would as quickly disappear, in that faraway silent storm.

ON OPPRESSIVELY HOT SUMMER DAYS the stone library building in our town offered the cool surroundings of a cave, and Dale and I frequently went there together. One afternoon as we made our way home, we stopped under the shade of our juniper tree fort behind the Courthouse. We climbed onto our usual seats upon the low candelabrum-like branches. I reached up to pull a couple of silvery-blue berries from the tree, as was my habit, and pierced them with my fingernail to release their dense aroma. Dale and I braced our feet against the rough trunk and tilted our faces to look up at the sky. There, billowy clouds were being pulled together as if by the force of a giant magnet. In fascination, we watched them sweeping upward into an immense tower, flattened on its top. The tower did not remain plain in color; it soon began to glow as if enchanted, with tints of peach around its curves that spread and ripened into a deep orange.

"Oh, that is the prettiest cloud I've ever seen," I said.

"Yes, but you can bet a storm is coming," Dale replied. And she was right. Taller and taller grew the thundercloud until it touched the top of the sky dome and loomed above us like a large-headed goblin. A smoky purple painted itself in outline around the whole giant form and pierced each of its fluffy segments. As the sky ominously darkened behind it, the thunderhead began to glow from within, as if the monstrous goblin had snatched the sun from the heavens and swallowed it entirely. Now the great cloud turned itself bluish black, and a startling rumble of thunder warned us that we had better escape to better cover than our juniper tree. Large drops of rain began pelting steadily from the sky as the two of us stuffed our library books under our shirts and ran toward the street.

As we raced across the grass of the Courthouse grounds, we were startled by a brilliant flash behind us and a sharp snapping sound. We whirled around to see one of the lawn's tallest junipers split by lightning. Dale and I screamed like banshees, then just stood, shocked, and stared at the smoking branch that had fallen to the lawn. We had crossed that spot of grass just seconds before. Our eyes met and we both blew out a sigh of relief, then we tore across the rest of the lawn and down the street to Dale's house. We were not quite soaked to the skin when we reached shelter.

"That burning tree was like the one Moses saw, the one sent by God," declared Dale.

We were now safely settled at her kitchen table, both of us clad in dry shorts and shirts from her dresser. Our dampened library books were spread open across the table to dry, and Dale's mother had just brought us cups of cocoa and a plate of cookies.

"Maybe. But that seemed more like the work of The Devil to me," I said. We considered that theological point while we munched our snickerdoodles.

Being good little girls of Scandinavian ancestry, we never missed Sunday School and church services at the large Lutheran Church in the center of our town. Our teacher in the Sunday School class was Mrs. Thornstad, a reverent, righteous, middle-aged woman of stern countenance who wore baggy, opaque brown stockings, not tight, see-through ones like our mothers wore. Her voice was nasal and she always sang much louder than anyone else in the congregation and unfortunately far off the designated key. It was clear that during the hymns Mrs. Thornstad was possessed by a private feeling of transcendent harmony with the Lord and so, oblivious to those mere humans standing near her, she let her phlegmy voice soar thunderously, rapturously, to connect with her Savior. During Sunday services, a person could pinpoint through the rows of crowded pews exactly where this woman was located by the loud atonality coming from that section of the church. Her singing could throw off even those members of the congregation who knew they had perfect pitch.

One Sunday morning as I sat in her class, Mrs. Thornstad expounded on her beliefs regarding Sin. She had announced in a prior lesson that we were all sinners, children as well as adults, but on this day she elaborated at length how each and every one of us intentionally or heedlessly committed several sins every single day. She listed the Seven Deadly Sins for us, and she told us that committing small sins could lead up to committing the more deadly ones, and therefore, even the least of sins could be considered as shameful as the greatest. "Now," said Mrs. Thornstad, "we will each talk about a sin we have committed. Who will be first?"

Not one of us children raised a hand. I thought hard. I knew I had not committed any of the Seven Deadlies, at least not recently. Sometimes I had been guilty of Envy toward my younger sister Katie whose hair was flaxen and formed itself naturally into perfect sausage curls, considered by all to be much prettier than my own straight brown locks.

It was true that I had committed Gluttony at times by secretly eating chocolate chips out of the bag in the kitchen cupboard, and then when Mother asked why there weren't enough of them left to use in a batch of cookies, I had committed the sin of Lying when I said, "I don't know". And taking them from the cupboard in the first place was the sin of Stealing, so that would count for three sins actually, if I had done that recently, but I had not.

Lying was one of the lesser sins, but a serious sin nonetheless since it could lead to the Seven, and I had probably lied by not telling Dad about all those matchbooks I had dropped in the dirt during his campaign stop in Dagmar. But that sin, and those others had taken place a while ago.

I had not recently conspired with Alex to swipe a box of Mother's Jello and eat it raw with licked fingertips or over ice cubes, which would have been Stealing, Gluttony, and possibly Lust

I did not really understand what Covetousness involved, how it differed from Envy, so I hoped I had not done that. I had certainly not committed the sin of Pride. I had nothing to have Pride about except my shiny tap shoes, and I couldn't really have too much Pride in that regard because all the other girls who had attended Miss Dottie's School of Dance had them too.

Sloth was something that was virtually nonexistent in our town, a community where the very idea of attaching porches or to houses was frowned upon. Even Two-Louse, who did not have a paying job, was constantly occupied with his sweeping and he was never slothful. I could not sit still long enough to commit Sloth since there were simply too many things to do outdoors.

The sin of Anger was a little less clear. I felt Anger at times but it always went away before I did anything mean. Outward expressions of Anger, such as those exhibited by the Three Stooges in the movie shorts, involved chaotic pummeling with fists, kicking, and harsh grunting and yelling. I never did anything like that when I was angry; surely it was not a sin just to feel Anger.

A heavy silence filled the room. Mrs. Thornstad's gaze passed around the circle of wooden chairs, pausing for a moment on each clean-scrubbed face. Her severe expression remained unsoftened. She was waiting for some young sinner to answer her question and she was not going to continue the lesson until that happened. The long silence became unbearable to me and I fidgeted in my chair. And then impulsively my hand shot up into the air.

"Yes, Jeanne, go ahead."

I took a breath and my words came pouring forth "I have not committed any sins today and I cannot think of any that I did yesterday either. I'm not sure, but I think maybe I have not committed any sins for a couple of weeks."

The silence in the room was absolute. Mrs. Thornstad looked intently at me for a long moment as she tried to figure out what kind of creature sat before her. At first I thought she was wondering how this little girl, I, could be so good, so unsinful, and she was thinking of a way to praise me for my exceptional goodness and proper Lutheran deportment. But as she continued to scrutinize my face, I began to suspect that she was judging me in a different manner. My face began to feel warm. At last Mrs. Thornstad was inspired with the perfect answer for such unholy impudence.

"Well, Jeanne, you may think that you are without sin, but you have committed a sin just now by claiming that you have not sinned today. You are telling a lie if you say you are without sin, and that lie you are telling is clearly a sin. **You are a sinner.** We are all sinners here on this earth, and if you think you are not a sinner, you are committing one of the Seven Deadly Sins, one of the worst, that of Pride. Remember, 'Pride goeth before a fall.'"

Every child in the class, even my best friend Dale, stared at me and I, of course, turned beet red. My face felt so hot that I imagined in my shame and guilt that I might suddenly burst into a pillar of fire, one burning so intensely that it could lead other sinners through the open wilderness of the northeastern Montana prairie. Across the land for forty years we would wander, probably west toward Redstone, and then a deep cleft would open in the earth, and all of us sinners would free-fall right into the flames of Hell. As that whole scenario passed through my brain, I did not lift my eyes above the rounded lumps of my own knees. After what seemed close to All Eternity, the Sunday School class ended.

While I waited in the hall for my sisters to come out of their Bible classes, I kept thinking about Mrs. Thornstad's words. In the couple of years that I had been attending Sunday School I had been very worried about Evil and the powers of The Devil. Because Satan lived deep below the earth and had tremendous strength and otherworldly powers, I always imagined that He could rise up from Hell and pass through the slightest opening in the ground to come right into our world and seize us sinners. I had been terrified about going down into Grandma Christina's cellar by myself, afraid that with a loud clank, the drain cover below her old-fashioned wringer washer would move aside and through the opening, I would see the red horns and hooded head of The Devil as He emerged from below and began to hoist Himself out of the sewer. When He saw me, He would snatch me by my feet and drag me down into Hell. I had seen a cartoon in the *Great Falls Tribune* that illustrated what happened there below. Crowds of tormentors, all identical Devils with goatees and pointed tails, stoked the furnaces and pushed the sinners into them. Although I knew that I was looking at a cartoon, there were many narrative details that supported a factuality apart from the intended humor of it.

As I had grown older I had finally overcome my fear of Grandma's basement by deciding that Satan might not be able to squeeze himself small enough to get through the particular drain opening there. The discussions about Evil and Sin still alarmed me, though, and I was certain that I could never be good enough to escape burning in Hell someday. I knew that being in church did not give me the warm glow of "Perfect Peace and Understanding in the Grace of our Lord" that the Pastor and Mrs. Thornstad often described true believers as having. I was certain that I *had* experienced a warm glow of perfect peace on the night when Vinny and I had lain on our backs in the snowy field and gazed up at the sparkling heavens, but such an all-encompassing feeling of love and connection was something that I never felt in church. There in the designated house of worship I felt mostly sensations of guilt and shame. The Devil was more real to me than God was.

I sighed out loud, mortified that I had somehow managed to be caught sinning right there in Sunday School. Mrs. Thornstad always said, "We must eschew Evil," emphasizing the "choc" syllable so it sounded very much like a sneeze. Unfortunately, I had not managed to eschew.

Vinny and Alex came out of their classrooms, and the three of us went into the church proper to join our father in the second pew. The service always started with the familiar hymn, *Holy, Holy, Holy*, sung as the choir filed through the church and up into the choir loft. I found that the singing was the only pleasant part of the church service and *Holy, Holy, Holy* had some of the prettiest words of all the hymns. I liked how at the end of the verse the congregation hissed like snakes:

All the S-s-s-saints adore thee
Cas-s-s-s-ting down
Their golden crowns-s-s-s
Upon the glas-s-s-s-sy s-s-s-sea

A Mighty Fortress Is Our God, written by the founder of our church, Martin Luther, was another of my favorite hymns to sing. The music was simply majestic as the organ player emphatically pounded out the chords and the whole congregation sang:

A Mighty Fortress is our God,
A bulwark ne-e-e-e-ver f-a-a-a-ail-ing

I liked how the strong sound of the words fit the hammering beat of the organ. I enjoyed singing the word "bulwark," although I was never quite sure what a bulwark was. It seemed like it could be a large ferocious animal or even an especially gigantic granite boulder. The "fortress" part reminded me of some of the snow forts my sisters and I had built and then my mind traveled to the lovely winter landscape. During church I always found outdoors things to think about, and this made the length of the service more endurable. The droning voice of the Pastor continued on and on during the sermon, and when I interrupted my daydreaming to tune back in to his voice, trying to determine if he was near to finishing, I would inevitably find that he was saying the same things as before, always talking about sinning and repenting and forgiving. It was so confusing to me that I doubted whether I would ever find the perfect peace and understanding, the grace, to get myself into the pearly gates of Heaven.

But the doubters were few in Plentywood, and probably ninety-five per cent of the population would be worshipping contentedly on a Sunday morning at our main Lutheran Church, or at the Methodist, Congregational, Presbyterian, Missouri Synod Lutheran, or Catholic churches. The Seventh Day Adventists and the Holy Rollers, located on opposite fringes of the town, did their worshipping on Saturday nights.

⟨≈⟩

ON WEEKENDS DURING THE SUMMER Dad took us picnicking and swimming at Brush Lake. Mother sometimes stayed home with the toddlers, and while the little ones napped, she could work on her oil paintings in her basement studio. But it was most fun when the whole family piled into our black Chevrolet to drive the forty miles to the lake, traveling south on the blacktop past Reserve, then east on gravel roads which circled farms and passed by areas of rolling prairie. Coming over the last rise of hill, Brush Lake lay shimmering ahead in a silver and blue mosaic under the summer sky.

There were groupings of tall poplar trees scattered around one end of the lake, and with the wind rustling softly through their leaves, the little groves made pleasantly cool picnic areas. Our family always brought the same picnic lunch of Mother's delicious fried chicken, potato salad, radishes, carrot and celery sticks, and lemonade to drink.

A beach of coarse sand edged the south rim of the lake, and the crowds of swimmers gathered there to spread out their towels before venturing into the refreshingly cool water. At one end of the beach a weathered wooden building once used as a resort was still standing. The main part of the building was a large dance hall /roller rink when our father was in high school. One wing of the building had offered a few small rooms for overnight lodging, and another wing had a restaurant and cocktail bar where the younger patrons tried to look old enough to drink alcohol. On weekends live music was presented, and the use of the ballroom's wooden floor would alternate between roller-skating and swing-dancing. Teenage boys from Plentywood borrowed their fathers' cars to drive out to the lake on Saturdays. Young men and women from the surrounding farms and small towns came to make new friends and be sociable with those they already knew, safely out of sight of their parents.

Then World War II came along, and when many of the young men of the area went off to fight for their country, the small resort went out of business. By the 1950's the only part of the building not boarded up or in partial ruin was the wing where the restaurant had been. Now this space housed a snack bar and small tavern.

A broken pier stretched out into the lake, its grayed boards a souvenir of the booming days when rowboats were tied up there for rental. Dad, called Bud back then, and his high school pals rented the little skiffs and rowed out into the deep water of the lake to drink their beer, then they filled the bottles with lake water to make them sink to the bottom. Out in the middle of Brush Lake was submerged a small mountain range of amber glass beer bottles.

One Saturday in August, Dad, Vinny, Alex, and I had spent a pleasant afternoon at the lake, and as the sun lost its burning heat and sank westerly, we girls floated lazily on our dull black inner tubes. We had already swum several times as far out into the lake as we were allowed, a distance measured by alignment with a lone poplar tree standing halfway up the North Dakota side of the shoreline, and so we were content to just drift on the gentle waves pushed along by wind.

That time of year, the shore was a medley of muted earth tones when drying grasses and weeds assumed the colors of the pebbles and sand. Dragonflies hovered at the edge of the lake and offered small flashes of color in the dull surroundings as their shiny emerald or royal-blue bodies flitted among the sparse rushes. As I watched their movements, I thought that to be a dragonfly would be a grand life. You would be a creature of whims—sometimes traveling in the air; sometimes touching down on earth or water; always darting and floating on delicately sparkling wings.

Dad called to us from the shore, "Time to get out and dry yourselves, kiddos. I'm going to the snack bar for some cigarettes. Be back in a few minutes."

Vinny, Alex, and I paddled into calf-deep water, then stepped carefully over the pebbled lake bottom and onto the gritty beach. We dried ourselves, then each took a turn changing out of her wet bathing suit and into her shorts and shirt inside a makeshift tent made of towels held up by the other two girls. When we had changed, we rolled up our wet suits in our towels and sat in the sand waiting for our father. He did not come out of the building after several minutes had passed, so Vinny fetched a long stick from underneath one of the poplar trees and she began sketching out a big map in the sand. Alex and I joined in, making the map topographical by digging out valleys and rivers and piling up handfuls of wet sand for mountains. We all remained engrossed in expanding our Sand Land until we noticed that our built-up mountains were beginning to cast shadows. The sun was getting low in the sky, slipping close to the bare wooden skeleton of the old dance hall at the far end of the beach.

Still Dad did not appear in the doorway of the snack shop, so we decided to go look for him. We picked up our wet towels and inner tubes and trudged across the sand. As we reached the old building, the pink neon BAR sign flickered and lit up in one of the windows. Through the dark tinted glass we could see our father seated on a stool at the bar. We moved close to the window and watched him talking and laughing with the woman who worked there. She had her elbows propped on the counter and she was leaning close to our father as they talked. After a little while she noticed the three of us at the window and tapped our father on the arm and pointed in our direction. Dad waved gaily, took a last swallow of his cocktail, and then came out the door. He stumbled slightly on the broad wooden step and tilted backward. The doorjamb steadied him and he lit up a cigarette as he leaned on it.

"Okay, kiddos, a-l-l-l-l-l-l-l aboard, let's go."

Vinny and Alex exchanged a solemn look, then each took up a position on one side of our father as we started to walk to the Chevy. I followed along behind, sniffing the sticky alcohol smell clinging to Dad and blending with the acrid smoke of his cigarette.

The ride back to Plentywood seemed to take twice the usual time. As we traveled the gravel roads Dad sang many of his regular songs, but he vibrated his voice into a crazed imitation of his usual singing and he even mixed up the words to his favorite hymn, *The Old Rugged Cross*. I looked at my father's face in the rear-view mirror whenever his singing paused, and I thought I saw his eyes droop shut once or twice. I glanced over at Alex at the other end of the back seat, and through the dusky light it looked like she was crying. When the car reached the blacktop for the last half of the drive home, Dad started smoking again, one cigarette after another.

Mother came running out to meet the car as we pulled up to our house.

"What happened? I've been so worried…."

"Nothing. The girls were having such fun swimming that we stayed a little late, that's all," said Dad. "What's for supper?"

A strange expression passed over our mother's face and I felt a knot of uneasiness inside of me. I looked at my eldest sister, and Vinny returned my look blankly. There was nothing to be said.

AN ARTFUL KIND OF MAGIC was produced in the dull concrete basement of our house where Mother had set up her painting studio. She hung old sheets from the ceiling to divide off the area for her workspace and she placed her large wooden easel just below the windows which let in the natural light of the north. Beside the easel she had a table to hold her brushes, palette, and oil paints. Piles of rolled-up, crinkled metal paint tubes looked like a miniature wrecking yard, and many had cracks which exuded a honey-colored sap where the linseed oil had separated from the thick pigment. A dense, exotic smell came from the split tubes, and the heavy fragrance intensified when Mother was painting, filling the basement and permeating the floorboards above her studio with a redolent reminder of the creative work occurring below.

I liked to read the names of the colors, sometimes spelled "colours," on the crumpled tubes. The unfamiliar words had fascinating, mysterious names: burnt umber, cadmium red light and cadmium yellow deep, madder lake—why was it called madder, I had to wonder, was it more angry than other lakes, and if so, did the anger make it into a dark pink color rather than the usual blue of water—and Hooker's green, and Van Dyck brown. And who were Hooker and Van Dyck, and why were paints named after them? If it was because they were great artists, then our mother should have a paint color named after her, too, I decided, and if she did, it would most certainly be a bright and dark red shade, the color of the lipstick that she wore. It would be called Lorraine Red Deep.

Once, while our baby brother and sister were taking their naps, Mother sat us three older girls in a pose to paint our portrait. She had dragged an old sofa to a spot facing the windows and then placed us where our faces would glow with the reflected light. From our positions on the sofa we could see framed sections of the blue sky through the windows, and that gave us a sense of confinement there in the gray-walled basement. We wiggled and shifted and could not sit still, until finally Mother just sent us outside to play. She later posed us for a photograph, and from that she was able to paint our group portrait.

Mother sometimes worked on still life pictures, gathering and arranging the objects in her studio, then observing them carefully as she painted. One such arrangement included fresh tomatoes from Walter's garden, with a sheaf of tall yellow prairie grass and golden wheat stalks in a canning jar, and a blue tablecloth spread below. The little painting captured the brightness of summer with its vivid primary colors. Horses seemed to come to life in other paintings of hers, and landscapes were a favorite subject.

The landscape paintings she had created when she first came to Plentywood reflected her interest in the vast spaces surrounding the town. She had depicted the prairie flats and rolling hills, the limestone buttes, the farmland fields, and the creeks with sparse stands of cottonwoods. After living for a few years in the area, however, her focus changed and she left those quiet scenes for more tumultuous worlds in her paintings. She began to create landscapes with surging mountains and ripped-open chasms, violent skies over tempestuous seas, and dark jungles made of writhing plants and deep shadows. Maybe those were scenes she remembered from her early travels; maybe they were places she still longed to see; maybe they were imagined.

The latest works had thickly painted surfaces with broad slashes of color defining the forms, and gashes of her palette knife cutting through them, much in contrast to the tamely brushed washes of diluted color in her earlier paintings. The strangeness of these vistas fascinated me. One time, I asked Mother if she was painting a scene from a fairy tale.

"Yes, dear, I guess I am," she said without looking up from the colors she was mixing.

"Which one?" I had to know.

"Not one from a book," was her answer.

VINNY AND ALEX WERE GIRL SCOUTS and when they attended the meetings and outings, their absence left me without my most constant companions. Then I was expected to play with our younger sister Katie who was not nearly old enough to hike around the golf course hills. Her favorite activity was changing the nightgowns and bonnets on her slew of baby dolls, and that bored me quickly. I felt trapped playing with dolls inside the house when outdoors there were sunny skies and fields of tumbleweeds.

One afternoon when Alex and Vinny were at Scouts, I saw Dad collecting his fishing pole and creel. I begged to be taken along to the lake to watch him fish.

"It wouldn't be fun for you," Dad said. "You would have to stay quiet so you don't scare the fish away, and there's not much to do up there."

I really did not want to engage in another everlasting session of dolls that day so I persisted. "Please take me with——I can just watch. I can be quieter than a mouse. Please, Daddy."

My father relented and said that I could join him. He was smiling as he put on his tan-colored fishing hat, and I looked with admiration at his deep dimples. I was thrilled that just the two of us were going off together. With our big family, I rarely got to go anyplace with just Dad and no one else. We had shared an exciting adventure when we were trapped in the blizzard that one winter, but on other adventures there were always at least Vinny and Alex along. Maybe something as sudden and exciting as the blizzard would happen on this fishing trip— maybe it would be a tornado.

The two of us took the highway north to the grain elevator and few clustered buildings that formed the community of Raymond. Dad stopped at the tavern to buy some beverages for our lunch. Apart from the elevator, it was the largest structure in the town, built the size and shape of a barn, but with a bar's usual entry shed built onto one end to keep wind drafts away from the drinkers within. Dad came out with a large bottle of beer and an orange Nehi, then we drove to the small lake that was just beyond the town.

While my father fished, I collected pretty pebbles at the edge of the water and laid them out in patterns on the ground, forming a community of dwellings for passing insects and tiny creatures that I imagined. When the rocks dried out and began to look dull, I would splash more water on to re-brighten them. I walked along the rim of the oblong lake looking for wildflowers, but all I found were weed-flowers that looked like tiny yellow daisies but lacked stems for holding in a bouquet. I picked several of them anyway and placed their stemless blooms around my pebble town for decorative foliage.

Dad was not catching anything, and after a while he decided to quit for the day. He packed up his fishing gear, and I selected a handful of the prettiest of my stones, and put them in the pocket of my jeans.

"Want some potato chips, kiddo?" Dad asked me as he steered the Chevy into the dirt parking lot of the Raymond bar.

"Sure!" I replied. I was pretty well famished after spending the afternoon walking around the lake and looking for things to amuse myself. Potato chips were a treat, not purchased very often by my mother, and I loved their salty, greasy crunchiness. Dad went into the barn with the blue neon Hamm's sign in the window and I sat alone in the car. After a good amount of time had passed, I decided that Dad must have met some friends to talk to. He seemed to know almost everyone in the county. I wished I had brought a book with me because there was not much to look at there in the parking lot, and I knew I was not allowed to get out of the car.

Suffering from boredom, as well as hunger, I distracted myself by playing the Monster car game, ducking down onto the floor each time a vehicle passed by on the road, which was not a frequent occurrence in Raymond. At first the eyes of the sporadic Monsters were unlit and not glowing yellow, but as dusk settled in and headlights were turned on, the Monsters became more menacing. The sky slowly darkened and I became afraid to watch for the bright approaching eyes and the disappearing red tails as the rare Monsters traveled the road. I crouched low in the front seat and waited, rising up every once in a while to peek anxiously at the windowless entry shed of the bar. Occasionally a man would emerge and climb into his pickup or car, and each time I felt keen disappointment that it wasn't Dad.

At last the door opened and the dim light illuminated my father's old fishing hat. As he got into the Chevy, I noticed that he was carrying two things, my promised bag of potato chips and a little flat bottle, which he slipped into a front pocket of his slacks. The familiar smell of Dad's drinking filled the car as we drove home, and my father smoked his cigarettes as I hungrily chomped the potato chips.

At home, Vinny and Alex had not returned from the scouting trip so supper was delayed. After I set the table for Mommy, I went to get a book from my bedroom and I was startled to see Dad in there. He was pushing something under the mattress of the big bed I shared with Katie.

"What are you doing, Daddy?"

"Oh, it's nothing, kiddo, just a little secret. Let's not tell your mother, okay? She doesn't need to worry about everything."

I nodded. Mother did seem to have way too many things to worry about.

"It was fun to have you as my little fishing partner today," he added, smiling at me with his dimples as he left my room.

I closed the door behind him and crouched down to stretch my arm as far as I could between the mattress and box springs of my bed. I could barely reach the bottle that was there, but I stretched until my fingers encircled the neck of it and I pulled it out. It was the little flat bottle Dad had gotten in Raymond, and it was about two thirds full of golden brown whiskey. It looked like thin maple syrup as I tilted it up to catch the light. I felt a sinking feeling inside. I had heard my parents arguing several times about Dad drinking whiskey. He used to buy whiskey frequently, the type that came in the purple bag so perfect for carrying marbles, but he had stopped drinking it at the time of his last campaign. I knew my mother became very upset when Dad drank whiskey, so I carefully slipped the bottle back under the mattress and pushed it as far away as I could. I took my Reddy Fox adventure into the living room and stretched out on the floor to read. Soon Alex and Vinny came bursting in the front door, faces flushed with excitement. Their Scout troop had gone horseback riding at a ranch outside of Flaxville.

Supper was served up, and as I took my place at the table I thought I could still smell a hint of whiskey coming from my father. During the meal Vinny and Alex were full of lively conversation about their wonderful day and I was quite jealous of their experience. It was my dream to ride a horse by myself, a beautiful pinto like Gramp's Gypsy.

Mother was very quiet and seemed to watching my father. I was afraid that she, too, was smelling the odor of whiskey on Dad. When supper was finished, the others left the dining room and I helped my mother clear the dishes away.

"I have to ask you something, honey," said Mommy. "Did Dad buy something to drink on your trip today?"

I hesitated and took a moment to answer and then I thought my voice sounded strange, more high-pitched. "He got himself a bottle of beer and an orange bloat for me."

"Anything else? Did he buy some whiskey?"

I looked away from my mother. I didn't want to lie to her, but I really didn't want to get Dad in trouble either. He had asked me not to tell my mother, not to worry her, and he had called me his little fishing partner. I didn't answer.

"Where did he put the bottle?" Mommy asked.

"I wasn't supposed to tell...."

"Sweetie, it's not good for him. I need to know where he put it. I looked in the car, and it's not there, so I know he brought it in. I checked the linen closet and it's not in there either."

I looked down at the floor. The brown and ocher colors and the stone-like shapes of the kitchen linoleum always interested me because they lent themselves to imaginary crossings on stepping stones across a river, but now I couldn't focus my eyes on them; they had become a blur of gray.

"You don't have to tell. Just show me where it is," said Mother.

I led her to my bedroom and lifted up the bedspread and pointed at the space under the mattress. My mother reached in and pulled out the flat bottle. It was more than half empty.

Mommy carried the bottle into the bathroom, closed the door, and poured the rest of the whiskey down the sink. From outside the room I could hear the loud clink as the bottle hit the bottom of the metal waste basket. Suddenly Dad was there in the hallway, looking furious, his cigarette clenched in his teeth. He flung open the door and charged into the bathroom, then slammed the door shut behind him. The loud voices of my parents made me plug my ears as I stood helplessly in the hall. I felt sadder than I had ever felt before, and I waited there to tell my father that I hadn't meant to give away his secret about the bottle of whiskey.

Abruptly, the door sprung open and the door knob banged hard against the linen closet.

"I swear I will leave you if you don't stop!" Mommy cried out.

Dad lurched into the hallway, his ugly expression and red complexion so different from his usual handsome face that he seemed a different person. I wanted to explain what had happened, but when I saw his face I could not say anything. My father was holding his cigarette between his fingers and as he passed quickly by me, his hand darted out and the end of the glowing cigarette seared into the skin of my forearm. I had never felt such cruel pain and I saw the mark of a perfect little crater in my arm, a deep and strangely white circle against the color of my skin. Tears spilled down my face as I held my arm away from my body, staring in shock at the angry wound.

"What happened?" Alex came running up.

"Dad burned me with his cigarette," I sobbed.

"Well, you know he didn't mean to. It must have been an accident," Alex said.

"He did. He did mean to. I saw how he looked at me."

Alex went to get a band-aid from the medicine cabinet. As she stretched it over my burn, she said quietly, "You know that Dad, the real Dad, would never do that on purpose."

Through my tears I looked at Alex and tried to understand what she meant.

Harvest

IN AUGUST THE FIELDS of grain became a crazy quilt of sun-colored patches. Expanses of golden wheat and copper-orange barley spread out next to the pale yellow prairie grass. Dirt roads formed borders between the vivid sections, and rabbitbrush appeared as a decorative edging with its blooms of sandy ocher. Interspersed here and there, equally happy in fields, roads, or ditches, deep-yellow sunflowers fluttered languidly with the passing wind.

Hordes of grasshoppers leaped out of range of the pickup tires as Walter and his granddaughters drove the bumpy road to Old Lonesome. An abundance of the bounding pests could be expected to spread through the fields each year as harvest season approached, but one summer the usual grasshopper population exploded into Malthusian proportions. Legions of them encircled the almost-ripe grain fields.

At the homestead it was not possible to walk across the open yard between the shanty and the quonset without smashing several of them with each step. Vinny did not really mind; indeed, she would tread deliberately upon the chitinous creatures, relishing the sound of them being crunched beneath her sneakers. Alex and I found both the sound of contact and the consequence to be unpleasant, and we hopped about clumsily as we tried to avoid stepping on them. The jerkily moving insects struck at our legs as we walked, and the larger ones leaped high enough to smack smartly against our bare arms. The smallest grasshoppers were a pretty shade of lime green, but the bigger ones were dusty beige and ugly, very fearsome-looking with their large heads and gigantic eyes. They hid secret wings which were pleated like little fans, dusty black with a yellow stripe, and when they opened those wings they could spring in arcs high enough to slap hard against the skin of a girl's face.

We had a pet duck, Lucky, who lived at Gramps farm, and we liked to catch the pesky insects to feed to him. It took practice to sneak up and cup your hand over a temporarily idle grasshopper, then carefully scoop your fingers around its body to imprison it in your palm, using just the right pressure to hold onto the squirming creature without smashing it on the way to Lucky's pen. The duck would snap the delicious live tidbits from our hands right into his bill, scraping and tickling our palms as he grabbed the food. One time, I skillfully caught an especially large grasshopper for Lucky, a superb speciman that stretched across my entire palm as I carefully closed my fingers around it. I made my way toward the waiting duck. Suddenly, I felt a sharp pinch in the soft fold of skin between my thumb and first finger.

"Yee-ow!" I yelled. I opened up my hand and there was the awful insect tightly cleaving to my skin. A pool of brownish red liquid was smeared across my palm.

"Help!" I screamed. "I'm bleeding!" I shook my hand violently as I tried to loosen the grasshopper's grip. The nasty thing would not let go. "Vinny, get it off!"

Vinny tugged at the pinching grasshopper but it still would not let go. She twisted its long body away from its head, and with a little crackle, it snapped apart and fell from my hand. She looked at my wound and laughed.

"That's not your blood, Stupid," she said. "It's tobacco juice. Grasshoppers spit out tobacco."

I rubbed the sticky juice onto my overalls and looked at my hand in amazement. The little mark from the pincers was still visible on my skin and it felt tender. To me, grasshoppers had always seemed rather like jumping safety pins, with their oblong shapes and variety of sizes, but now there was another resemblance: the pain of being pricked by one.

LONG-LEGGED, RACING JACK RABBITS and demurely hopping cottontails had thrived in eastern Montana for ages before the wave of emigrants arrived, and the lagomorphic population continued to outnumber that of the humans. This was partly because of the animals' prolific procreative habits, and partly because of their tan-colored fur which kept them successfully camouflaged on the arid prairie.

The balance shifted somewhat during desperate economic times when the hardscrabble farmers and ranchers in the area became predators of the quick-moving creatures, joining the coyotes and sharp-eyed hawks who preyed on them regularly. Then their numbers decreased. Through the fairly prosperous 1950's the feral rabbit population was large and stable, but toward the end of that decade the natural order of things was shaken up when a new variety of rabbit was introduced into the countryside.

This happened after our father returned from an alcohol treatment program in the western part of the state. There he had chanced upon a feed store as he was looking for a late Easter present to bring to his children, and he was immediately taken with the Black Giant rabbits on display. With their sinister coloring they presented a rather diabolic image of the Easter Bunny, and the gift was perhaps analagous to bringing coals to Newcastle, but we were delighted with them.

The oversized rabbits, a male and a female, were kept in a hutch outside of our house, sheltered somewhat from the never-ending wind by the propane tank. We called them Licorice and Midnight. Before long, a batch of ten wriggling offspring magically appeared. The newborn babies first resembled miniature pug-nosed hippopotami, but they quickly grew long ears and became adorable bunnies with ebony fur as soft as silk. Their growth rate proved to be phenomenally fast and when the rabbit children began to reach the size of their parents, it was clear that more space was needed for them. Dad decided that the family of Black Giants should be transported to our grandfather's homestead and released into the Coulee.

My sisters and I begged shamelessly to keep the dozen rabbits there in our yard. We had given them all names and we could tell them apart even if our parents couldn't. Dad told us firmly that they were bound for the farm, named or not. We then pleaded to keep just a couple of the babies but Mother said absolutely no. My sisters and I reluctantly helped Dad load the hutch into the back of Gramp's pickup and off to the farm the Black Giants went.

After a short time, major changes were seen in the established feral rabbit population on the prairie. Peculiar markings began to appear on the bodies of newborn cottontails and jacks. The black patches contrasted strikingly with the rest of their beige or gray coats and resembled the random sloshes you might get from a dropped bottle of India ink. Some of the bunnies were neatly brindled all over with tiny drips of black. There were those with large circular blots on their backs, like clownish polka dots, while still others sported whimsically shaped splotches in odd places on their bodies. We saw one speciman with a unique variegated shading. It was divided by black and beige colorings roughly down the middle of its back. This gave the animal the strange semblance of a flattened rabbit hopping along and carrying its own shadow with it.

These distinct new forms of coloration surely placed the rabbit population of northeastern Montana on a grafted branch of the evolutionary tree. We do not know for certain whether our former pets and their descendants continued to flourish. Perhaps the rabbits hid more easily from predators with the inclusion of shadowy patches on their fur; perhaps that was not the case and they became clearer targets under the bright sun of the northern plains.

WHEN WHEATFIELDS WERE PRIME for harvest around Grandpa Walt's place, he finally drove his big combine out of the quonset. It was freshly tuned up and oiled. The hauling truck also emerged from the cavernous structure, sometimes with the three of us girls perched on the cracked leather seat in the cab beside Gramp. Dad joined the work crew to help his father, taking time from his office in the Courthouse to spend long days in the fields.

Hard at labor, the Minneapolis Moline traveled on a rectangular track, curving at the corners, around and around the golden sea of grain, its big slicing paddle chopping off the wheat stalks in a wide swath. The combine's orange color blended harmoniously with the surrounding grain and was vivid against the deep blue sky. When in motion, it was like a self-contained dust storm as it continuously blew clouds of chaff and dirt in its wake. After several circulations, when its cylindrical tank was filled up, the combine paused to rendezvous with the wheat truck and shoot the load of stripped kernels into the truck's open back.

Vinny, Alex, and I liked diving into the back of the partially filled wheat truck for a pretend swim, joining the live or dismembered grasshoppers already floating in the loose grain. The feeling of thrashing through the load of wheat, arms flailing and feet kicking, was similar to swimming except that no real forward propulsion was possible through the grain without kicking off from the sides or bottom of the truck. It was a fun but filthy activity. We were coated from head to toe with the fine grittiness of wheat dust when we climbed out of the truck, and we had mismatched pieces of the chopped-up grasshoppers all over us—the angled legs, thoraxes, and big-eyed heads clinging to our shirts and pedal pushers and filling up our pockets. We were only allowed to play in the grain when the truck was not moving. We could not ride in the back of the full wheat truck when it was driven to the granary for unloading.

The old Mary Olsen granary was close to some of Gramp's wheat and barley fields, but it no longer housed anything but nomadic rodents. Back at Old Lonesome, Gramp had two new circular granaries made of shiny metal, as well as an old wooden rectangular one that resembled a house without windows.

His long-necked grain auger had been pulled over to the wooden granary one day in the middle of harvest, and we girls watched as it slowly sucked a load of wheat right out of the back of the truck and blew it through a small trapdoor into the granary. Beside the trapdoor opening a narrow ladder was built onto the outside wall of the whitewashed building. Vinny liked to see how quickly she could scale the ladder almost to the roof. As soon as the empty truck headed back to the field, she climbed up the ladder to peek inside the building. She discovered that several other truckloads of wheat had already been deposited, and the mound of grain came to within a few feet of the angled ceiling.

"Oh, this will make great swimming," Vinny said. She called down to us, "I'm diving in!"

"Do you think it's okay?" Alex asked.

"Why can't I? Nobody told us not to. Come on!" Vinny insisted.

"The water's fine!" She disappeared into the granary.

Alex climbed the ladder and I followed. She and I and squeezed through the square opening and crawled in on top of the grain pile. We saw Vinny rolling on her stomach and paddling her arms in swimming motions.

"Come on in," she called to us. "It's so fun!"

We hesitated.

"Scaredy-cats!" Vinny taunted. Just then the grain shifted slightly and her body started to sink down under the wheat. Her legs were no longer free to paddle-kick.

"Come back, Vinny," Alex said, scared. The grain beneath us seemed solid enough, but we hung back closely against the wall.

"You swim out to here," Vinny answered. "We'll have a race when I get my legs out." But as she turned sideways to talk to us her body sank even further into the pile. The wheat was shifting all around her, pulling her lower. She tried to reverse herself to swim back toward us, but when she moved again, the pile swallowed more of her body.

Now Vinny had just one arm and shoulder completely free, and the grain was coming right up to her chin. Her eyes showed her sudden alarm.

"Don't move, don't move anymore!" Alex screamed. She looked around the walls and at the rough four by four support beams crossing between them, and she saw what she should do.

"Okay, Vinny, don't move until you can grab my leg." She held onto the beam right above her and extended her foot as far as she could, but not far enough for Vinny to reach.

"Wait. You have to help me, Junior."

I didn't know how I could do anything. I was really scared.

"Okay, Junior, I'm going to hang onto your foot and you have to crawl out to grab Vinny's hand. Go slow. Real slow."

I didn't want to. I might sink down into the wheat too.

"You can do it," Alex said.

Alex stretched her arm around the beam and grabbed firmly onto my ankle with her free hand. Slowly, I extended myself out across the grain. I was a lightweight and I didn't sink into it. Finally I was able to clutch Vinny's hand with both of mine. Vinny had been uncharacteristically quiet but now she urged, "Pull hard. Hurry up."

Alex did. She pulled on my skinny ankle with all her strength and it hurt like crazy, but she was strong and she moved me toward her as I pulled Vinny. Then Alex grabbed onto my pedal pushers, and then my shirttail and around my waist, and she tugged with all her strength to drag both of us back across the unsteady pile of wheat.

As the three of us were climbing down the ladder, Dad saw us from the other side of the farmyard. He called us over to the quonset to give us a good scolding.

"Don't you *ever* go in there again. I mean it. That grain will suck you down like quicksand," he told us. "You could suffocate in there."

MY SISTERS AND I liked eating kernels of wheat at harvest time, not the dusty grains stripped out of their heads by the combine, but the ones gained by picking a yellow stalk straight from the field. It was necessary to pull apart the stiff whiskers to separate the little pockets of kernels, then the papery covers were unhusked to find each oval grain. The ripe wheat had to be ground firmly between the molars to soften its hardness but then it tasted good. Even better, I thought, were the kernels picked earlier from green wheat stalks. The unripe grains were milky inside their thin green wrappers, sweet-tasting and chewy.

As wheat and barley became ripe, many of the good vegetables were ready to be harvested too. Gramp and Dad took pitchforks to dig up the potato patch at the farm, and as they broke the soil and lifted the dark-green plants out of the earth, Vinny, Alex, and I scrambled around with burlap bags, each trying to collect the most red-skinned potatoes. When I found very small ones, I slipped them into my pocket rather than throwing them into the gunny sacks. The marble-sized potatoes were delicious to eat raw, with the clinging dirt adding to the flavor. Cooked, they were pretty good too, especially when our mother made creamed new potatoes and peas. We picked the long rows of corn, then shucked some ears to be boiled and eaten fresh, but most of the crop was blanched by Mother, then wrapped in brown paper and masking tape, and frozen for eating in the winter. Yellow waxy beans, peas, and green string beans she wrapped in neat packages too and stacked in the freezer. The giant tomatoes grown at the farm were as sweet as could be, which made it seem odd that Grandma Christina sprinkled her tomato slices with sugar before setting them out in a crystal serving dish on the table. She said it was a custom in her family; Norwegians liked to have their tomatoes sweet. Gramp said Swedes did too, if they were as sweet a tomato as she was.

Near the end of harvest in the area, a Pioneer Days celebration was held, and the citizens of Plentywood dressed up in the style of their Scandinavian forbears: long dresses and bonnets for the women, and not really much of a costume change for the men, perhaps a red or navy blue bandana added around the collar of a cotton shirt or hung out of the back pocket of denim jeans, and a different hat. Felt or straw cowboy hats were dusted off for a special appearance, replacing the faded and sweat-stained long-billed caps usually worn by farmers. Many men grew whiskers and entered the beard-growing contest, judged by popular vote of the citizens. That was one election Walter Janson chose to enter.

We granddaughters enjoyed running our fingers across his stubbled cheeks as Gramp's gray beard started to grow, but we shied away from touching it when it became longer and bushier. Then it resembled a small, prickly porcupine snuggling up against his neck.

I really wanted to help Gramp win the vote for Best Pioneer Beard so I spent several hours one day drawing on typing paper, creating posters to spread around the town. I followed the design of Dad's County Attorney campaign messages, showing a crayon picture of Grandpa Walt with his bristly beard and a cowboy hat in the middle of each poster, and the words **ELECT JANSON** above his face and **DEMOCRAT** below it. I was thumbtacking a poster to the telephone pole on the townside corner of the county hospital property when Vinny and Alex approached on their way home from a Girl Scouts meeting.

"What's that, Junior?" my sisters called out.

"A poster to help Gramp win the election," I replied.

The two of them looked puzzled. "What election are you talking about?"

"The Pioneer Beard election, of course," I answered. Vinny and Alex were probably wishing that they had come up with the idea of making campaign posters for Gramp, I thought. But then I could see that they were laughing.

Vinny started to say something about Democrat beards, but as she sorted through the stack of papers, she snorted with laughter and couldn't finish. Still laughing, she galloped across the hospital grounds toward home.

Alex looked at the scattered posters on the ground. She saw that I had spent a lot of time working on them. I had varied the color of the cowboy hats and hatbands from poster to poster, using most of the crayons in my box. The beards had been carefully drawn with many strokes of my gray crayon to distinguish the textural bushiness.

"Are you going to put all of these up?" she asked.

"Yes, so Gramp will win the election."

"Then I guess you might need a little help," said Alex.

She and I trotted around the streets of our town and tacked the posters to fenceposts, utility poles, and gates. No one else had bothered to put up posters for the election, I found as we worked.

My campaign efforts must have been effective because Gramp won the Best Pioneer Beard election by a landslide. After the votes had been tallied up, the whole town gathered at the fairgrounds for a ceremony to announce the winner of that contest and to award prizes for the largest home-grown vegetables and the best home-baked goods. For the occasion, Gramp wore a brown felt cowboy hat, a red-and-white-checked shirt, faded denim pants, and the leather vest and chaps from his cowboy days. He looked very distinguished with that prickly beard. In front of everyone, he was awarded a giant blue satin medallion with ribbon streamers and a silver-tipped bolo tie. We granddaughters cheered raucously as Walter climbed up onto the wooden bandstand to accept his award but the next day we were most happy to see his tanned face smoothly shaven again.

On the final day of the festival, as women carried away their ribbon-winning pies, pickled vegetables, and crocheted doilies from the exhibit hall at the fairgrounds, the enormous orange harvest moon rose grandly into the deep indigo sky and beamed a golden blessing onto the prairie town. Then men waited eagerly for hunting season to begin.

MOST MEN IN THE COUNTY were avid hunters, stalking the fields of harvested grain and stretches of prairie grass for pheasants, grouse, deer, and antelope, or staking out the cattails of Medicine Lake or the Big Muddy Creek for ducks. Walter Janson had never enjoyed hunting but his son was fond of the activity, and Dad combed the fields of the homestead for game birds and deer. Despite his enthusiasm, my father was not especially accomplished at shooting animals. Occasionally he did manage to bring down a duck, a couple of grouse, or a pheasant. When those strong-tasting wild meats were roasted and served with mashed potatoes for a Saturday night supper or a Sunday dinner, we girls thought they were poor substitutes for our mother's delicious fried chicken.

My sisters and I liked to ride with Dad in the Chevy when he set out on long forays into the countryside in search of the ideal gathering places for prey. Sometimes he traveled north past his father's farm to the acres Gramp owned near Outlook, where rolling hills were broken by pale limestone formations. Sometimes Dad hunted near Archer, an isolated olden settlement with just a name and a single structure left standing, the tiny one-room schoolhouse that he had attended as a boy.

We were never allowed to get out of the car when our father left with his gun, and the three of us would crouch on the floor by the back seat and use the upholstery as a table to play card games. We played Old Maid, with colorful circus performers printed on the cards, and my sisters would conspire and take especial delight in sticking me with the eponymous spinster, a sinister-looking, bespectacled woman who must have been in the audience at the circus; she clearly was no performer. And we played Authors, another pointless game of pairing cards, but victimless anyway, the object being that doubles of bushy-bearded, white-mustachioed, or long-haired men, and Louisa May Alcott, be matched up, game after game.

One afternoon we started on a hunting trip by heading north of town, then we took a gravel road west from Raymond towards Outlook. All of a sudden we were witnesses to an event of startling loveliness as we passed a common field of cut hay. There, hundreds, maybe thousands, of swallows had gathered to rest, hidden from our view in the stubbled grass. The little birds, perhaps roused by the sound of our car, took to flight suddenly and rose from the field in splendid array, their numerous small bodies shimmering in the sunlight as they came together in a great lifting spiral. Dad slowed the car to a stop as we watched the birds, then we continued along the road. I turned around in the back seat and got up on my knees. I kept watching the swallows through the back window until they were out of sight, trying to understand how those birds could form themselves so swiftly and perfectly into that silvery helix. It was a miracle of light and grace.

We drove into an area where the flowing prairie dropped off into cutbanks and coulees and Dad pulled off the road. He let Vinny go with him as he scouted around the area. Then he came back to the car to get his rifle, and Vinny climbed into the back seat to play cards with Alex and me. We played a couple of games of Authors, then Alex dealt out Old Maid. We were sorting through our cards when all of a sudden a shot cracked brittly over the near hillside, earsplitting and startling in its finality. A momentary pause, then the echo of the shot sprang from the canyon as an incongruously cheerful whistle.

"Dad must have shot his deer," Vinny declared. I stared at her. She returned my stare with a knowing look.

"It was a deer he went after?" I asked.

Vinny told me that when she and Dad had checked around for signs, he had pointed out little round balls of deer scat among the pebbles in the dirt. The droppings were fresh and he thought the deer must be close by. She had known what he was hunting and had been eagerly anticipating the sound of Dad's gun as we played our games.

"You mean he killed it?" I said, incredulous. I had been on many hunting trips with my father, but most often he failed to shoot anything and returned home empty-handed. Occasionally he had gotten a bird or two, but once retrieved, they were quickly stuffed into a burlap bag, so I had barely glimpsed their limp, feathery bodies. The main part of a hunting expedition had always been the ride in the car; the killing part was not in the realm of my experience. And I had never imagined that Dad would actually shoot an animal as big and interesting as a deer. Whenever our Chevy startled a grazing deer on the way to Gramp's farm, the graceful creature would raise its neck to gaze at the big black intruder, then she would dart away through the grass with such agility and elegance that I thought there could be no more beautiful animal in the world. Surely Vinny was mistaken. Perhaps Dad had not really shot a deer; perhaps he had just fired at another pheasant.

Now he appeared over the crest of the hill, walking briskly with his rifle pointed down and a huge grin stretching across his face. "I got her!" he called out.

"Yay!" Vinny yelled as she jumped out of the car. "Can we see it?"

"Yes. You're going to have to guard her for me. I need to go get Walt's pickup to carry it back to the farm. Who wants to stay with Vinny?" He looked at Alex and me.

"I will," I said. I wanted to see the deer, to see whether it was really dead. Maybe it was only wounded and then I could do something to help it get away before Dad came back. My father placed his rifle in the trunk and then led us over the hill.

"There, girls," Dad pointed.

The deer was lying halfway down the slope.

"Just go and wait there by my deer. We'll be back in half an hour," our father said.

As Vinny and I approached the fallen deer, I could see its eye was wide open and a thrill of hope shot through my body. It must still be alive. I stood and watched as Vinny walked around the deer and looked carefully at the little round bullet hole in its chest. Only a trickle of blood stained its light brown color.

"See, it's a doe," she said, "because it has no antlers." She completed her inspection of the animal, then she sat down on a flat granite boulder to wait for Dad.

I knelt by the perfectly still animal and looked at her long neck curving across the smashed grass. At the end of that neck the doe's head was tilted awkwardly with one side pressed firmly against the ground. I waved my hand slowly in front of the deer's topmost eye, so liquid and soft brown, but it did not move. The animal seemed to be gazing past me and way up into the everlasting sky. With my fingertips I gently stroked the light fur along the curve of the doe's long face.

"Pretty deer," I murmured as the tears began to run down my cheeks. "Such a pretty deer." I leaned forward and kissed the snout of the doe. The deer's fur was very warm against my lips, and for a moment I believed that Dad and Vinny were wrong and it could not really be dead. Still, the doe lay perfectly motionless.

"I'm so sorry that Dad killed you," I whispered. I sat in silence beside the doe until Dad returned.

Gramp came with his son, driving the pickup behind Oscar's Chevy. Alex climbed out of the car and came to sit on the rock with Vinny. I knelt down by them and the three of us watched as our father got into the pickup and drove it down the slope of the hill, steering around large stones, then backing up to within a few feet of the doe's body. Dad pulled open the transom, then the men took hold of the deer's legs to hoist her into the back of the truck. I held onto Alex's hand as we watched them load the dead animal into the pickup bed. The beautiful deer was thrown in like a bag of rubbish on the way to the dump. Never again would this deer have a home on the range or play under skies that are not cloudy all day.

Back at Gramp's homestead, Dad lashed the deer's forelegs together so they could hang her up for butchering. As they raised her onto a rope stretched between the grain auger and the quonset door, the deer swayed back and forth and then she spun around like an absurd ballerina with her arms looped over her head and her feet posed en pointe as they hung downward. Dad knotted the rope into place.

Our father had a large hunting knife with a leather-wrapped hilt and this he brought out to use on the deer. We had seen this fearsome knife many times, but never used for this purpose. Dad removed it from its dark leather scabbard and began to sharpen it on Gramp's old pedal-driven whetstone. Alex and I could not bear to see what was to happen next to the deer so we went into the shack, but Vinny stayed to watch. She was always interested in new information, and this time it was the science of butchering.

An old iron-framed bed filled one of the two rooms in the shanty, and Alex and I stretched out on its faded counterpane to play SORRY. A couple of games were enough to bore us, so we began flipping through yellowed copies of *LIFE* magazine, looking for pictures of Jane Russell, Marilyn Monroe, and Elizabeth Taylor. Then we amused ourselves by bouncing on the sunken mattress of the ancient bed until the coiled bedsprings and iron bedposts groaned in misery. Catching a glimpse of the sky through the small window of the shack, Alex noticed that it had turned dark outside. "Let's see if it's almost time to go home," she said. "I'm really hungry."

The two of us stepped out of the shack. Across the yard, a grisly scene was starkly illuminated by the pickup's headlights. What remained of the poor dead deer was still hanging there in the night, but the light beige fur and the flesh of its underside had been pulled away and terrible bright colors showed in its open belly: scarlet red, maroon, yellow, and blue. I gasped and covered my mouth with my hand, fearing that my own insides would churn up in disgust. I would not have known this gruesome patchwork to be the remains of the doe, except that her gentle head was still attached. The eyes of the animal were wide-open and lovely, transcending the ugly slaughter below.

A FEW DAYS after the hunting trip, I helped set the table for supper and I was happy to see that we were having one of my favorite meals. Our mother sometimes made a drive-in restaurant supper with thick French fries, hamburgers, and homemade chocolate milk shakes. I watched Mother blend the milk and chocolate ice cream in her largest mixing bowl, then she allowed me to carefully ladle up the frothy shakes into glasses and carry them one by one to the table. She served up the French fries in a huge bowl and placed the hamburgers on a platter. We all sat down to eat. Hamburgers were a rare treat, and I hurried to stretch some dill pickle slices across the meat patty, drizzle on the catsup, replace the bun top, and take a big bite of the special food.

"This tastes different," I said.

"That's because it's venison," stated Dad.

"What's venison?"

Vinny and Alex exchanged a look of amusement, eyebrows raised.

"It's deer meat," Dad said. "You're eating a deer burger."

A big lump arose in my throat and I could not swallow the bite stuck in my mouth. The lump grew bigger and I thought I would choke. I opened my cloth napkin and tried to be discreet as I spit the mouthful into it. My father saw me.

"We do not waste food in this house," Dad said sternly. "There are millions of people going hungry in the world. You are going to eat the rest of that meat. Every bite."

I stared at my plate. I had never felt less like eating anything. Even the French fries looked like they would stick on the lump filling up my throat. But the deer burger would choke me. It was that beautiful doe—it was poison.

I often got into trouble for refusing to eat things that everyone else liked. Breakfast was the worst. Cream of Wheat always made me gag and especially because I would stall and let it sit, desperately hoping that it would magically disappear, but instead it congealed into a thick white quicksand that was impossible for me to choke down. A fried egg always reminded me of a giant eye. The yellow middle would stare rudely at me as I carefully cut the white section into bites, rubbery triangles that I could swallow whole and barely taste. But then the gluey yolk, the worst part, was left there detached on my plate. I could not bear to have it even touch my mouth. When I looked at the hated circle I wondered how people could stand to eat something that was as slimy and yellow as the blood of a squished fly. I would finally escape from those dreadful breakfast foods when it became time to walk to school with my sisters. Mother would relent and remove my dishes. But it was clear that my father was not going to let me leave the table without eating the deer burger. I felt trapped in my chair. I nibbled on part of the bun so it would seem like I was obeying Dad.

Other family members were enjoying the venison burgers. Vinny and Dad each ate two, and even Katie and Johnny in their highchairs were eating most of the patties cut into bites for them. I kept thinking of the doe's large eyes and soft fur and I knew that I would not eat a bite of that meat even if I had to sit there forever. While I considered whether there was any way for me to escape, I made myself chew on some of the cold French fries. They tasted like library paste.

At last, everyone got up from the table except me. Mother and Alex cleared the dishes and began to wash them. The gnawed-on hamburger bun on my plate did not hide the uneaten meat patty, and my father looked intently at it as he left the room.

"You are going to sit there until you eat every bite," he said. He went into the living room to read a bedtime story to his two youngest children.

In the kitchen Mother and Alex had almost finished with the dishes.

"How are we doing?" Mommy called out to me from around the room divider.

"Not quite done." I pushed the plate away and rested my head on my crossed forearms. A plan of escape occurred to me. Maybe I would sit there until everyone went to bed, then I could sneak out to flush the venison away in the bathroom. But, no, that wouldn't work because Dad would never go to bed until he saw that I had eaten the meat. There was no way to escape from that terrible non-hamburger on my plate.

A sudden whisper in my ear startled me.

"Junior, just eat the bun." Vinny quickly grabbed the venison patty and wrapped it in a piece of notebook paper she was carrying, then stuffed it in her jacket pocket. Whistling as she went, Vinny headed out the kitchen door and into the yard. I watched through the dining room window as Vinny walked across the street to pet our neighbor's Black Labrador, then I ate the soggy, catsup-soaked bun with the crisp pickle slices and I drank the last of my melted chocolate milk shake.

LESSONS

I‍T WAS THE WEEK BEFORE SCHOOL BEGAN in September. Children all over town were savoring their last happy moments of freedom in the sunny outdoors when they witnessed a phenomenal event—an elephant came lumbering through the streets of Plentywood. It's hard to imagine what could have been more unexpected. Few townspeople had ever seen an elephant outside of the pages of *The National Geographic Magazine*, and citizens of all ages ceased their activities to stand on the curb and watch the alien beast stride down the streets. It was a small elephant, not a baby but far from adult in size, and the upwardly curving shape of his open mouth made him seem to be smiling or even enjoying an unending silent laugh. The animal was accompanied by a trainer and whenever the gregarious beast slowed his brisk pace to look at the townspeople, the man would smack him smartly on the backside with a long thin stick. Some observers were horrified to see the little elephant thus abused, and others allowed that this was how an elephant was trained and he could feel nothing through his thick leathery hide.

The animal trainer had slicked-down black hair and was dressed very exotically for northeastern Montana, even judged by the standards of the Fancy Hat Lady. He wore flowing lavender trousers like a character out of *1001 Arabian Nights*, with a red vest around his shockingly unshirted chest, a tasseled fez atop his head, and high-ankled black basketball sneakers of the type worn by boys and my sister Vinny. The elephant had a threadbare gold and emerald piece of brocade spread across his back, edged in red tufted trim, but this cloth did not manage to conceal a long wound across his lower haunch. The deep slash had been treated with iodine, which gave a strange coppery shine to the elephant's gray skin around the wound.

As the curious spectacle of man and beast moved through the streets, it was joined by groups of children following almost trancedly along the sidewalks. Never, in anyone's memory, had a pachyderm marched through the streets of Plentywood. A few inhabitants of the old folks home attached to the hospital, who were sitting outside in the warm sunshine, rubbed their eyes in disbelief when the elephant and master passed by.

"Well, ain't that Something?" said more than one old fellow. Continuing around the block, the parade caught the attention of the outer neighborhood's softball players, and our marathon game, tied up at 26 points each, was halted.

"An elephant!" I shrieked the obvious from out in left field. Both teams raced to the street to better observe the amazing sight.

Now the trainer stopped, doffed his hat with a flourish, and bowed low toward the crowd on the sidewalk. "Come to the circus," he bellowed dramatically. Again, and even louder, "Come to the circus!" he commanded, modulating his deep voice with all the melodrama he could muster. He then struck the small elephant with a flourish of his stick, exclaimed, "Forward!" and proceeded onward past the hospital. Most of the softball players now joined the parade, including my sisters and me.

"Did you see that poor elephant's wound?" Alex asked.

"Yeah. It's a known fact that a trainer has to beat an elephant to teach it tricks," said Vinny.

"Really?" I could not believe that anyone would hurt that jolly elephant on purpose, but Vinny was rarely mistaken about anything factual.

The elephant and master were traveling at a good clip, and we scurried to keep up. When the crowd reached the county Courthouse, the exotically dressed trainer directed his charge to turn right and they continued south through the downtown. Patrons of the post office and shoppers at the Red Owl grocery stopped to stare in wonder at the creature from far-off India marching down the Main Street of a small Montana town. The trainer now paused at every street corner to urge the crowds, "Come to the circus!" before parading on.

At the town's major intersection, where Main Street crossed First Avenue, the procession suddenly stalled. There came Frode Larsen driving his old blue tractor, a tremendously noisy piece of machinery that was alternately moaning in agony and sputtering in breathless gasps, and all the while burping out greasy cloud puffs through a vertical exhaust pipe. The elephant stopped and studied the contraption crossing his path. Frode braked his rig and ground to a halt too. Prairie farmer and exotic beast stared intensely, each unflinchingly at the other. The crowd of citizens on the sidewalks watched the stand-off between modern civilization in the shape of Frode on his tractor and primitive animality in the form of the pachyderm. Which creature would yield the road? A few moments passed, then the smiling elephant took a step forward and trumpeted loudly toward the sky. The blast of sound reminded older citizens in the crowd of the Model T horns heard when automobiles first came to Sheridan County almost a half century before, and people began to smile and chuckle.

"Well, I'll be jiggered," Frode said, then moved his rig backward with great resonating shakes of the aged engine.

"Forward!" ordered the trainer, and the elephant marched triumphantly past the tractor to follow First Avenue out to the county fairgrounds.

Gramp and Grandma Christina decided to take their three oldest granddaughters to see the circus. A carnival with rides and game booths sometimes came to town during the harvest festival, but people could not remember the last time an actual circus had performed in town, nor could anyone predict when such a cultural opportunity might appear again. The circus was held in a large square tent made of patched canvas that had been erected on the fairgrounds. The performance stage was a circle in the center of the tent that was demarcated by a ring of straw bales. The audience members sat on wooden bleachers set up on three sides of the tent, and the fourth side had a large hanging tarp to conceal the comings and goings of the various performers.

Clowns entered the arena first and their very appearance made the eager crowd applaud thunderously. Two clowns pulled a baby carriage into the ring, and when the baby emerged from the buggy, he was much larger than his parents. He picked up the mother clown and carried her away, revealing her big polka dot-patterned bloomers, and the audience roared with laughter.

A number of other acts followed, and each seemed more thrilling than the last. A woman stood straight up on her white horse to gallop around the big circle, then she rode sidesaddle and hung dangerously close to the ground as the horse traveled even faster.

A black-haired cowboy who very much resembled the elephant trainer performed skillful rope tricks with a huge spinning lasso. Vinny was spellbound, noting the subtleties of arm movement he employed to keep the rope turning continuously. She would remember those rope-twirling positions to try later.

His act was followed by a remarkable spinning woman who wore only a skimpy yellow bathing suit and was suspended by a rope from the center of the tent. She held on to a small hoop at the end of the rope, and she made graceful poses with her legs like a ballerina, then she turned herself upside down and placed her feet through the hoop. She stretched her arms straight below her head, then began twirling her body slowly, then faster and faster until finally the form of a woman disappeared altogether and she became just a blur of pink and yellow.

Three jugglers astonished the crowds by skillfully tossing and flipping several bowling pins, then large rings, and finally breakable plates, before becoming acrobats to flip and toss themselves through the air too. They used a seesaw board to catapult and somersault dangerously high above the ground, and they ended by stacking themselves up on one other's shoulders to form a single giant man. The man on top was recognized by us to be the elephant's trainer, and Vinny whispered, "He was the cowboy rope twirler too," and I gasped in amazement.

There were apparently no limits to the man's talents because he appeared again after a short act by the clowns. This time he wore a safari costume as he directed a real live bear into the center of the tent. It was a black bear wearing a ballet skirt around her middle, and one of her legs was attached to a long chain. After she ran a lap of the ring on all fours, the trainer yelled something at her and swiped the bottom of her backside with his long stick. She rose onto her hind legs and circled the tent walking upright like a person. She was as adorable as a stuffed teddy bear, and the crowd clapped enthusiastically.

As the final act of the circus, the little elephant appeared wearing a red feather plume atop his head and a gold and red cloth across his back. A woman in a sparkly red bathing suit was mounted upon him, her legs wedged right behind his ears, and the audience's noisy appreciation of this duo surpassed all previous applause. The black-haired trainer, once again garbed in his *Arabian Nights* finery, was holding a rope attached to the elephant's collar and he led them slowly once around the ring, and then began to run. As the elephant picked up his thick legs and trotted quickly around the center of the tent, the woman bounced up and down like a crazed ping pong ball. Then she slid off the elephant's back and bowed to the crowd, over and over again as if she, apart from the elephant, had done something remarkable. The citizens of Plentywood apparently agreed that she had, as their wild clapping reached new levels. Now the elephant climbed up onto a big wooden box, and goaded by his trainer's voice and a light touch of the long stick, he shifted his weight backward and slowly, slowly lifted his forelegs into the air. The tent erupted with a sound like mid-July thunder. People pounded their palms and stamped their feet on the wooden bleachers, and some boys and farmers whistled through their teeth. It was the most extraordinary sight one could imagine on a warm September day in northeastern Montana. The little elephant standing on his hind legs was truly Something.

WHEN THE PLENTYWOOD SCHOOL opened its doors the next week, children were still buzzing with the excitement of the circus coming to town. Before the first bell rang, boys and girls were trying to duplicate on the playground some of the amazing circus feats they had seen, and many a student entered the new year's classroom with a bruise, scrape, or bloody nose.

I was eager to join the fourth grade class of Miss Mary Bergstrom, a warm-natured Norwegian woman who had taught both of my older sisters during their fourth grade years. The night before, my mother had swirled my straight hair into pin curls, placing the bobby pins in precise Xes around the sides of my head, and now a soft corona of fluffy waves caressed my shoulders and bounced lightly as I walked into the red brick building. Wearing my favorite dress, a blue plaid with a white collar, and my brown MaryJane shoes, I stepped purposefully on the green and gray checkerboard squares of linoleum leading down the long hall toward my class.

I was carrying my school supplies: a thick writing tablet; a pencil box containing three pencils, a six inch ruler, and a spare eraser; and a new box of crayons. For the first time, my mother had bought me the largest-sized box of Crayolas, 48 in all, and now I slipped open the box to look at my treasure. In neat and vibrant lines the 48 colors sat lightly wedged in their places, like rows and rows of avid spectators seated in bleachers, each wearing a colored dunce cap and each waiting to be chosen to make a bold mark across a piece of white paper. Which one would I choose first? I loved the bright pure red so I might choose it, but then again, no, I might keep its smooth point intact for as long as possible. The sunny yellow shone out at me, and I imagined pressing it very firmly onto the paper to make the clean, light color dense enough to show up. As I enjoyed the idea of coloring with those brand new crayons, I nearly bumped into the open door of Miss Bergstrom's room. I closed the box and stepped inside the classroom, full of happy expectation.

Miss Bergstrom welcomed me and assigned me to a desk near the front of the room. I glanced over my shoulder to find Dale, and the two of us waved our greetings. Then a large object above caught my attention, and I looked with amazement at the giant globe suspended a couple of feet below the high ceiling. That globe was to captivate and educate me like no other object of my early years.

The globe was raised and lowered by a rope and pulley. Over the years it had explained the seven continents and seven seas to many generations of fourth graders. The writing on the globe was in an old-fashioned script, and the earthen colors representing the various countries evoked the past too: moss green, yellow and red ocher, faded burgundy, and umber. The touch of exploring fingertips during decades of use had located and lightened the central section of many a nation. The oceans were not blue as logic would prescribe, but tinted in an ivory shade. The ancient-looking script and the antique colors of the globe conjured up a feeling of mystery in the far-off lands and long-ago times described by Miss Bergstrom in her lessons, a world of wonder beyond the boundaries of Sheridan County. Lovely and intriguing names were called forth from the globe, names like Tierra del Fuego: the Land of Fire, Sahara Desert, Island of Madagascar, Outer Mongolia. Miss Bergstrom showed her students how Hannibal and his army rode their elephants on a daring journey through the treacherous Alps Mountains. Few of the children in our class had ever traveled as far west as Butte or beyond Bismarck in the other direction, but the globe carried us to places that were strange and fascinating.

Miss Bergstrom taught arithmetic, grammar, science, and social studies with a Scandinavian thoroughness, but her great loves were art and poetry. She plastered the walls with the colored drawings and construction paper projects of her students. She rewarded us for memorizing and reciting verse, and she encouraged us to write our own poems about the things we saw in our surroundings. Each Friday morning Miss Bergstrom opened the day with recitations and readings. For every accumulated one hundred lines of poetry she or he had memorized, a student was given a satin ribbon bookmark, and the girls especially strove to collect one of every color. The poems we had written were also presented to our fellow fourth graders. Each poet would stand in front of the room to read the piece of work, and this was followed by polite applause from the class. All of those original poems were carefully collected and typed up by Miss Bergstrom for a thick book she had been compiling during her teaching years. She called her book *Serendipities*.

One school day in October a special subject for study presented itself. A dust storm blasted across the prairie from the east and roared through Plentywood. On the playground during lunch hour, children saw the ominously dirty clouds approaching over the hills and we heard a higher pitch in the whine of the wind. And then the turbulence was upon us. Strong winds carried huge fistfuls of gritty dust and hurled them every which way in a dirty fury. Hard particles slapped at our faces as we raced for shelter.

Back in our classroom, we emptied out our shoes and shook the loose filth from our jackets and sweaters into the waste basket. Each of the twenty-five children now had, except for variations in length, the same hair: a tannish brown color that was stiffened with dust into the coarse texture of a horse's tail. More dirt coated the insides of our mouths and noses. We took turns rinsing ourselves at the sink and then sat down at our desks. As the winds blew harder and the dust clouds grew thicker, the students could not look down at their readers. All attention was focused on the madly swirling dirt. The world outside Miss Bergstrom's classroom was a blizzard of brown; even the bright sun was blotted out by the clouds of dust. The playground structures twenty feet beyond the windows disappeared from sight. Dust forced its way through the closed windows' frames and drifted inches deep on the sills.

Practical Miss Bergstrom tried to resume the study of the English language, in particular how to parse a sentence, but she could not compete with the whirling dervish of a dust storm that was heaving itself against her room's tall windows. At last she moved away from the blackboard and intently watched the storm's fury for a few minutes. Then Miss Bergstrom spoke. "Boys and girls, just look at the power of Nature. What we are seeing gives us a special opportunity. We will end our grammar lesson and you may write poems about the dust storm."

Every set of eyes had been turned toward the windows but now girls and boys fished in their desks for their pencils and lined manilla tablets. Writing a poem about the raging dust storm was an exciting assignment and the pencils soon began to make scratchy noises across the pages. I loved writing poems and I quickly put my words to paper, pausing to erase only a couple of times. I wrote:

Dust Storm
Dust all morning,
Dust all noon
Dust until the evening moon.
My, this is a dusty time
Dust is in your book and mine,

Dust is on my paper too
Dust is in my sock and shoe.
What a dust storm!
What a wind!
Everything is in a spin.

Miss Bergstrom had cleared off a bulletin board, and now, as each student finished the dust storm poem, she promptly tacked it on the wall. Against the blue paper backing, our manilla sheets looked like remnants of the dust clouds that had blasted down upon us.

When the bell for dismissal rang that day, the winds had abated and the clouds of filth had settled, and children waded through drifted piles of soft dirt on the streets leading to their homes.

ON THE NORTHERN GREAT PLAINS fall temperatures cooled down suddenly and drastically, and when this happened, small creatures came to seek refuge inside warm houses. A nest of ten baby mice was discovered inhabiting a box of old clothes in my family's basement one day, and all of us children were delighted. The tiny pinkish rodents were nestled together in an old mint-colored cashmere sweater that our mother had worn in college, and the writhing mound of bodies resembled a quaking shrimp aspic just unmolded onto a bed of lettuce. Alex leaned close to study their squirming forms.

"Can we keep them for pets?" she asked our father.

"We could raise them for science experiments," Vinny suggested.

"Please let us keep them, Daddy," I begged.

"Mice are not really meant to be pets," our father said, "but we'll see, kiddos."

Vinny, Alex, and I went outside to play, but a little while later we went back to the basement to check on the mice. The nest was gone.

"Did Dad move them into the old rabbit hutch?" I asked my sisters.

"I don't think so," Vinny replied. "They would fall through the grating."

We returned to the street corner and started another game of HORSE at our makeshift basketball hoop, a stretched-out wire clothes hanger attached to the telephone pole. But then I noticed Dad walking around in the back yard so I ran over to ask him about the mice. He had started a roaring garbage fire in the burn barrel and now he was tending it with a stick until it died down enough to ignore. A pillar of eye-stinging smoke surged upward, with flat gray cinders swirling high into the clear air.

"Daddy, where are the baby mice?" I asked breathlessly.

My father stirred the fire and said, "Mice are not meant to be pets."

MISS BERGSTROM'S STUDENTS were given the assignment of writing reports about famous people they admired. I was fond of reading about people's lives, and I had already gone through the entire series of blue fabric-covered biographies in the children's section of our town's library. One of the first biographies I had read was about Benjamin Franklin. He had invented and created many things in his life, I found out, but I was most grateful that he had been inspired to found the first public lending library. I could not have imagined our town without that precious brown stone building on Main Street. Almost all of the biographies in the series had been about famous men, but two books had told the stories of famous women: Clara Barton, and Jenny Lind, the Swedish Nightingale. When I read about those women's lives, I had felt a strangely personal pride in their accomplishments, and I had read the Clara Barton book twice. I was considering one of those women for the subject of my report, but then I got a better idea. I decided to write about a famous man, a man I admired tremendously, and one of the leading citizens of Plentywood. I decided to tell the story of my grandfather, Walter Janson.

I wrote about his birth in a farmhouse in Minnesota, his childhood spent working on his father's homestead near Outlook, and the details of his leaving home when he was in the fourth grade, the same level as Miss Bergstrom's students, to go work on a cattle ranch. I related his adventures as a cowboy on the range, and I described the variety of other jobs he had tried before he became a homesteader. I described how smart my grandfather was: how he knew all about important things like farming, machinery, and weather, and how he also knew about small, useful things like the way to unscrew a tick.

I related how Grandpa Walt was well-known for his strength even though he was not a very large man. When he had worked in the coal distribution business he always delivered his loads much faster than anyone else. His secret was that he had welded a big piece of metal onto the largest size scuttle to extend its capacity, and being so strong, he could then carry bigger loads and make fewer trips to the customers' coal chutes.

I wrote about the fact that people were always asking Gramp to run for Mayor. I told of Walter's friendliness, the way he would greet a stranger as kindly as he would a fellow farmer. For the last sentence in my report I wrote, "Walter Janson is not really famous in other parts of the world, in places like Outer Mongolia and Switzerland, but he is very famous in our town of Plentywood."

When the reports were finished, Miss Bergstrom set aside a week to celebrate famous people and she had a few students read their reports to the class each day. At recess on the morning I had read my report about Gramp, I was climbing the monkey bars with Dale. Two of the girls from our class were climbing above us, and the one named Donna called down. "Hey, Jeanne, how come you wrote a report about your grandfather? He's not a famous person."

The other girl joined in, "My grandfather is way more famous. He's a doctor in Williston."

"Both of my granddads went to college," continued Donna. "Your grandfather must not be very smart. He only went to the fourth grade."

I stared at her. I quivered with Anger of the Seven Deadly Sins variety and I knew that Anger was not going to be dispelled without an outright expression of Sin. I had never tried to hit anyone with my fists except my older sisters, and only when they were being exceptionally mean in their teasing and then dared me to hit them, but now I felt like climbing up and socking Donna hard.

"My-y-y-y grand-dad is much smart-er than your-r-r-r-rs!" Donna added a singsong to her taunting.

I really, really wanted to hit Donna, but fighting was what boys did and then they usually got into trouble, so instead I snapped out with a forbidden phrase, "Shut up! Donna, you just SHUT UP! No one in the world is smarter than Gramp!" And I knew that was true.

EVER SINCE WE BECAME FRIENDS in the first grade, Dale and I had walked home from school together. During fourth grade we were sometimes joined on the walk by Billy, a boy from our class who lived a block away from me. Billy was the cutest boy in Miss Bergstrom's class. He looked like a brown-haired Howdy Doody with freckles on his nose and plumply rounded cheeks. His lips were redder than any girl's, and he reminded me of the barefoot boy in John Greenleaf Whittier's poem. I had memorized the first ten lines of the long poem for Miss Bergstrom's Friday recitation:

Blessings on thee, little man
Barefoot boy with cheeks of tan
With thy turned-up pantaloons,
And thy merry whistled tunes;
With thy red lip, redder still,
Kissed by strawberries on the hill;
With the sunshine on thy face,
Through thy torn brim's jaunty grace,
From my heart I give thee joy,
I was once a barefoot boy.

Sometimes when Billy walked with us girls, I found myself looking at his dimpled cheeks and thinking, *from my heart I give thee joy.* He was nicer than the other boys. When I wore my hair in braids he didn't tug at them, and he didn't try to stare up girls' skirts when we climbed on the monkey bars. He didn't talk very much but his grin was wide and he showed it frequently.

Dale and I liked walking with Billy, but when he tagged along with us we did not cut through the Courthouse grounds to stop at our special juniper tree fort. The fort was our own shared secret, so with him we would travel home by the sidewalk in front of the Courthouse. Dale's house came first on our route, then Billy and I walked the last four short blocks and the very big block around the county hospital. And sometimes Billy passed by his own house to go with me right to my yard.

One afternoon after the two of us said goodby to Dale we began discussing the Hardy Boys adventures we both had read. Arriving at my house, we sat down on the steps by the kitchen door. I could smell the chocolate drop cookies my mother was baking in the kitchen, but I could wait for them while I finished talking to Billy. As we pretended to argue about which of Frank and Joe's cases had been the most exciting, I saw that Billy's cheeks were rosy in the autumn air, his red lips *redder still* not from strawberries but from the cold, and he looked so handsome that I knew I wanted to marry him someday.

From my heart I give thee joy....

Suddenly I reached over and cupped Billy's cheeks in my hands, and leaned close to kiss him right on the lips. I felt the smooth softness of his mouth for only a tiny moment before Billy pulled back with a jerk, leaped up, and bounded like a frightened deer across the yard and into the street. He didn't look back and he didn't stop running until he reached the safety of his own house a block away.

I stood and watched Billy through bare branches of the tree in my yard, a young cottonwood Dad had transplanted from Gramp's Coulee. Before me a lone leaf remained, curled at its edges and hanging by an invisible gossamer, and as a breath of wind touched it lightly, it began to spin. Slowly at first, then faster and faster it twirled without apparent cause or effort until it became a blur of motion like the spinning circus lady, pure yellow against the cold blueness of the sky. I brushed a tear from my cheek and went into the house for some warm cookies.

CHANGE

O VER THE ROLLING HILLS and across the plains around Plentywood the prairie Wind is always present, even when its motions are not apparent. Then it is only resting or changing its direction. By design or whimsy the Wind shifts through various incarnations, and several of its forms may appear on a single day.

On pleasant, softly-scented days the womanly essence of the Wind reveals herself in movements of gentle swaying like a mother rocking her newborn. Sometimes she turns gaily with livelier gusts, like a sashaying square dancer as she circles her partner. This feminine embodiment of Wind is not only filled with grace, she is as mindful of duty as her human counterpart, and on a long day she can waft into dryness load after load of hanging laundry, and leave it sweet-smelling besides.

Another warm weather Wind is like a hardscrabble country mule with a disposition sometimes obstinate, sometimes impulsive, always contrary. Modern machinery has long since replaced the horse and mule as farm laborers, but the stubborn mule comes back to work as one form of the changeable Wind. This is most vexing for farmers to encounter on plowing and planting days. Sometimes the mulish Wind blows steadily for as long as the farmer works, persistently trying to disrupt the poor man's efforts, and then on impulse it might take a rest just when the farmer chooses to do so too. Or this Wind might remain still all day long, just watching while a farmer transforms his field of fallow into long, neat furrows ready for planting. Then, when all is ready, that mule of a Wind can take perverse pleasure in kicking up the light topsoil of the newly plowed earth and impetuously rearranging it.

The Wind is acting as an invisible sorcerer when he directs the effortless soaring of a hawk over the prairie. The very suddenness of a hawk coming into view is one of his acts of illusion, as if the conjurer wills the hawk to appear and so she is there at that moment. And the flight of the hawk—her endlessly long glides across an empty sky, and her impossibly motionless posturing aloft—these can only be tricks of a celestial Merlin, a force not seen but powerful. This Wind plays more modest tricks too, spontaneous little deceptions to amuse himself: he flutters the foliage of a poplar tree to send waves of light shimmering across it, and he breathes gently upon a still lake to cause a sudden lapping at its shore. And when this magician Wind seems to have just vanished, and the vast space feels perfectly at rest, then he might oh-so-lightly touch with a long finger only the seedhead on a tall grass to start it bobbing, making its movement a mystery when the grasses all around it are still.

When sundown comes and the last beams of light fade away in the west, a purposeful Wind pushes its way across the prairie. This never-failing presence sweeps down from the north; it is the Lutheran Wind. It blows with a sound of soft bleating and it blows with a devotion unceasing. It blows with a stern warning: beware the dark cloak of the night for it hides many sins under its cover. The Lutheran Wind preaches and whines all night long, then retreats into silence with the light of dawn.

At times an omen of Doomsday materializes in the shape of a demon Wind. This tormentor shrieks and groans and carries vile weapons to heave upon the earth: tons of suffocating dirt, wild hailstones, and black clouds full of slashing lightning. The Wind's attacks are sudden and ruthless but he soon moves on to other targets for destruction.

There is a Wind as shifty as Coyote. This cunning rogue sneaks and swirls across the prairie, playing tricks and causing chaos as he goes. He scatters loose debris, rearranges the order of things, and kicks up dusty clouds, then he hides himself in a canyon. The trickster Wind is fun-loving. He bounces tumbleweeds for miles and miles, and he sends little dust devils spinning through the fields like old-fashioned wooden tops. Then, when the Coyote Wind has enjoyed enough mischief, he lopes away and disappears over the next hill.

One of the cold weather Winds comes forth as a misty ghost. She rises from below the frigid, frosted land, from deep in the hidden hollows of a place's memory. Freed and airy, she floats over the wintry terrain, calling to her lost companions and loves. Her plaintive, distant cry comes echoing across the empty night spaces, a song of yearning for the things she has lost and tenderness for having had them once. The other Wind of winter is irrepressibly the spirit of the wolf, a creature who had long been a dominant presence on the prairie. The natural animal has not been part of the area's fauna for many years, but the lupine incarnation of the Wind reminds humans of the role that once was his. Now the wolf is heard again in the Wind that rages and howls when blizzards blow over the hills. If his cry holds a note of anguish, and if his roar seems vengeful, that is because he is remembering his lost brothers and sisters, those wolves slaughtered so mercilessly by the region's settlers over a hundred years ago.

ONE AFTERNOON WHEN the wind was in her female form, a zephyr fragrant with the smell of grass, Walter and Christina Janson picked up their four granddaughters for an outing. Little Katie was placed in between our grandparents in the front seat of their dove-gray Oldsmobile sedan, and Vinny, Alex, and I climbed into the back.

The three of us in the rear seat grabbed tightly onto the long velvet safety rope as we rode, and we pretended to be traveling at top speed over treacherous mountain roads in pursuit of spies. The Oldsmobile's actual journey was a little more mundane; it was headed for the badlands area north of Redstone where we would observe an oil well in action. Exploratory drilling had been going on for some time around the area, and now a small gusher had exploded right on the edge of High Pockets Peterson's northern sheep pasture. Gramp's friend was hoping that there would be enough oil on his land for him to strike it rich, and many other farmers and ranchers were also hoping their lands might yield a bumper crop of black crude. A foreman had already stopped by Old Lonesome to talk with our grandfather about the possibility of drilling into an exposed seam of shale on one of his hills. Oil fever was spreading throughout Sheridan County.

Katie was chirping happily in the front seat, and Gramp began to sing her special song:

K-K-K-Ka-tie
Beautiful Ka-tie,
You're the only G-G-G-Girl
That I adore
When the M-M-M-Moon
Shines, over the cow shed,
I'll be watching, waiting,
At the K-K-K-Kitchen door

Katie giggled and clapped her little hands together, and the three of us in the back seat let go of the velvet cord and joined in the applause for Gramp's singing.

The straight blacktop turned serpentine as we approached Redstone, and my sisters and I carefully surveyed the ditches and cutbanks for a possible fox-in-hiding. There were none that day. Just beyond the town, Gramp took the gravel turnoff toward the small community of Daleview. Now the roadside scenery offered a change. Deep gulches cut into the gentle grassy bluffs, and the pale limestone cliff formations were striped with lines of dark shale and wide strata of vermillion- and gold-colored sandstone. In places, the passage ran narrowly between steep hills, and the road surface became considerably rougher the further we went. "Ouch," said Grandma each time a loose rock clunked hard against the underside of the Olds.

Gramp drove slowly around the base of an impressive limestone rise, and then an amazing panorama opened up against the backdrop of the hills. The broad side of one bluff had been deeply sliced into and carved away to facilitate drilling of the oil on High Pockets' property. The naturally rounded slope of the hill had been straightened out to form a steep earthen ramp, and this wide swath of tannish dirt was bustling with the activity of an anthill. Giant trucks and a road grader were climbing and descending the ramp while they worked on extending the opening into the earth. The machines left zigzag-patterned tracks with their huge wheels in the soft dirt. Several sporadically spaced pumps were stationed on the scraped ground, all busily at work, and in their midst one tall metal tower commanded the hillside. The small oil rigs resembled half-starved horses seated on their haunches, heads and long straight necks bending down to earth, trying to take some food, then pulling up again to breathe, bending and pulling in constant, steady rhythm.

Gramp parked the sedan by the side of the gravel road. Many other cars and pickups had done the same, and folks were milling around and talking to their friends. Gatherings of this size were usually seen in Sheridan County only during the harvest festivals and celebratory church suppers. This turnout demonstrated that apart from the natural curiosity that folks have about something new— the oil drilling in their locality—the very idea of unexpected, unearned riches is irresistible.

Head and shoulders above the swell of the crowd, there stood High Pockets, the center of attention as folks asked him what he planned to do once he became a millionaire oil tycoon. High Pockets didn't have a ready answer so he just chuckled, shook his head sideways in amused disbelief, and chewed on his unlit cigar.

Grandma Christina sat in the car with Katie, who had fallen asleep on the way. This arrangement suited Grandma perfectly. The spotless interior of the Oldsmobile was far preferable to the filthiness outside. The rest of us got out and mingled with other curious folks. We walked up and down the dusty hillside, looking at the bobbing pumps and stopping to talk to Gramp's friends. High Pockets greeted each of us girls by our nicknames, then he reached into the paper bag he was holding and pulled out three pink bubble gum cigars. Our mother rarely allowed us to chew gum, and never in the shape of something a man would smoke, so the cigars were a treat. The three of us spent a good while pretending to smoke the gum before finally biting off some to chew. As we played in the piled dirt along the edge of the ramp, Vinny found a fist-sized, dark-amber agate. Alex and I searched for some treasure too, but all we found were small bits of mica. In late afternoon Gramp called us back to the car.

The sun dropped low toward the far western hills as the Oldsmobile traveled the gravel road back to the highway, and the bright blue sky faded into a bluish gray. Then other hues emerged in striated patterns of color like those in the cliffs we had just passed, but more intense. The yellow-gold afterglow of the sun ripened into tangerine and spread wide behind rose-saturated clouds. We watched the ribbons of deep pink intently, then they blushed into cherry red, as if they were suddenly aware of and embarrassed by their own startling beauty. Now the tangerine orange melted away like warmed sherbet, and dark lavender began to shade the sky. Striped together, the red and the purple formed a heavenly fabric that the Fancy Hat Lady would surely covet. Gradually, the bands of cherry color widened and lightened, then blew apart into puffs of pink cotton candy afloat in the darkening sky. Before our eyes, they diminished and sank until they become mere marshmallow shapes above the distant hills. Grandpa Walt drove along slowly as all the females in the car gasped, pointed, and sighed at the richness of the display. When the last of the clouds had merged with the night sky, we sat quietly for a while.

Around a curve in the highway the distant sparkling lights of our town became visible, and above them the sliver of a silver moon had risen. The moon seemed modest after the gaudiness of the sunset, but it promised us the same luminous glow on future evenings.

"You know you girls are too young to smoke," Gramp called out to the occupants of the back seat. "You'd better finish up those cigars before your mother sees them."

As the decade of the 1950's drew toward its end, an amazing invention was introduced into Plentywood—it was called television. One of the first television sets to arrive in town was purchased by Dale's grandmother, and I was invited by my friend to go with her to see this remarkable object. On a Saturday afternoon, the two of us dropped off our books that were due at the library, then walked to the Old Townsite to witness the workings of this modern technological wonder.

Grandma Johnston welcomed Dale and me into her small house and ushered us into her living room. The room was very dark with all the shades pulled down and no lamps turned on, but a whitish glow radiated from the screen of the television and flickered with the action of the program. The huge television console occupied much of the space of the tiny room, and its flashing black and white picture and blaring sound were immediately spellbinding. Dale and I sat down on the sofa and stared at the magic box before us. There it was, five feet in front of our faces, like a large old-fashioned radio set but with a picture too, so the people at home could actually see who and what were making all the noises heard over the broadcast. It was truly remarkable. It was like having the whole Orpheum Theatre shrunken down to fit inside Mrs. Johnston's living room.

Pictured on the screen, four sisters were singing in harmony. Each of the girls had perfectly cylindrical sausage curls, like my sister Katie's, with a huge ribbon bow atop her head. They were seated in a diamond shape, flat on the floor with the littlest girl in the front. Each girl had her palms neatly clasped together like she was shaking hands with herself. The girls' wide, gathered skirts were puffed out and hid their legs, giving them the look of singing cupcakes. As they sang the popular song *Sugar Time*, the girls tilted their heads randomly to the left or the right, then slowly the other way, all the while smiling so broadly it was hard to believe they could still be singing, and with such remarkable harmonization. Too quickly, the song was over and the sisters stood up to bow to the audience. Dale and I started to clap, then we giggled at ourselves for thinking that we should applaud when the sisters were not actually present in Grandmother Johnston's living room. A man with slicked-back hair appeared on the screen, clapping heartily and thanking the girls in his strange voice, calling them *The Lovely Lemon Sisters*. I was quite amused by their name. It really fit them because when the girls were singing and smiling so hard simultaneously, their faces were all scrunched up like they had been sucking on lemons prior to their performance. I wondered if my three sisters and I could learn to sing in harmony like those girls and then become *The Gorgeous Janson Sisters*, famous performers on the television.

AFTER SCHOOL ONE DAY, Dale and I made a quick trip to the library, then we walked back toward the Courthouse grounds to begin reading our new books in our fort. Halfway up Main Street, we were surprised to see my father leaning against the doorway of a building where he sometimes ate lunch. At that time of afternoon, he was always back at his office. I set my pile of books on the ground and went to see if my father was sick. As I approached Dad, his body slowly slid down the wall and stopped in a slump next to the stair railing.

"Daddy, what's wrong with ….." I started to ask, but I knew the answer as soon as I drew close to him. I could almost taste the dense sweet smell that clung to him when he drank a lot of whiskey, and as I inhaled that telltale odor, I felt sick myself.

A couple of years before, my father had gone away to a sanitarium in the western part of the state, and he had spent several weeks there to be cured of his drinking problem. Since that time my older sisters and I had sometimes smelled the whiskey odor, but we had kept that information from our mother because we did not want to upset her. When we traveled with Dad on his business trips around the county, or out to Brush Lake to swim, he often stopped at the small towns' bars to visit with the fellows, which was important for being re-elected to office, he always said. And when he emerged from those places, he was always very cheerful and brought us bags of salted peanuts or potato chips for a treat, and then he sang all his favorite songs on the way home. It seemed like his behavior was harming no one, and I personally felt rather proud that Dad would trust me, along with my older sisters, to keep the secret of his occasional drinking. The odor of alcohol which emanated from him when he came out of a bar would eventually disappear in his clouds of cigarette smoke as he drove us home. But there was no hiding that smell at this moment, and I hoped that Dale was not as skilled as I was in identifying its source. My father had been drinking in the middle of the day, and drinking a lot.

"My dad is sick," I said to Dale. "Would you take my library books to your house? I can get them later." Dale stared at my father, then without a word she piled my books on top of her own and continued up Main Street.

"Wait, Dale," I quickly yelled out. "There's Vinny. Would you tell her to come here?"

Dale nodded, and she ran as fast as she could manage under the load of books. She caught up with Vinny, who was walking in the middle of a crowd of boys who regularly escorted her home. "Your dad is sick," Dale panted. "Junior needs you to help." She pointed her forehead in our direction.

Vinny came racing up to where Dad and I were sitting on the steps. As soon as she drew near she understood the situation.

"Vinny, what are we going to do?" I wailed like a baby.

"Hi there, kiddos," Dad looked up as if he had just noticed he was not alone. "Time for me to go back to work." He pushed himself up from the step, but his unbalanced weight brought him back to sitting. He swayed forward as if to try again but this time he could not get enough momentum to make himself rise. He leaned back against the door displaying the words **VETERANS CLUB** in alternating red and blue block letters.

The name of the establishment was a little deceptive; it was actually a bar and open to anyone, not just veterans, who cared to partake of what Grandma Christina called Drink. The interior walls of the bar housed a display of photographs of the county's young men who had served in the armed forces. My father left college to join the Navy during World War II, and his picture in the Veterans Club showed him looking very handsome in the white dress uniform of an ensign. He had chosen the Navy because he, like his Uncle Rasmus, had always been fascinated by the idea of the measureless spaces of the ocean. Perhaps that was a natural consequence of having spent his whole life on the vast stretches of the northern plains.

Looking past our father sprawled on the steps, Vinny saw that our family's new car, a mint-green-and-white station wagon, was in the parking lot of the Veterans Club. "Help me get Dad into the car," she said to me.

We each maneuvered a shoulder under one of Dad's limp, heavy arms, and we slowly pulled him to a slouched standing position so we could walk him to the car. He was mumbling to us, with eyes half closed, and we knew that there was no way he could go back to the office in that condition. Two older ladies, friends of our grandmothers, were standing in the yard adjacent to the parking lot and they watched us unblinkingly, then they came close to the hedge to offer their assistance.

"No, thank you," Vinny answered, without looking over at the women. I could hear the buzz of their whispering from behind their hands as Vinny and I struggled past them and across the parking lot. I opened the door to the second seat as Vinny held our father propped against the car, then we both pushed and lowered him into the back. Now his eyes had closed all the way and we could hear his deep breathing. He must have fallen asleep.

"We've got to take him home," Vinny said. She reached over and fumbled through the pockets of Dad's suit jacket until she found his keys. "Get in," she told me. I stared at Vinny in disbelief.

"You're going to drive?"

Vinny was too young to have her driver's license, but she had practiced driving Dad's old black sedan several times at the farm, just those distances between the shanty and some of the fields. She had never driven the new Chevrolet station wagon.

"Get in," she repeated. I did.

Vinny started the ignition and pulled out onto Main Street. I could see the two women behind the hedge still staring as our car left the parking lot. Vinny drove slowly up Main Street to the stop sign by the Courthouse, there she carefully turned left. She kept her foot steady on the gas pedal and went very, very slowly. Fortunately, townspeople generally parked their cars in their driveways or garages but not on the street, so her way was clear. She scared me a couple of times when she scraped the tires along the curb, but she steered straight again, and Vinny brought our father safely home. Our mother was astonished and appalled. She and Vinny dragged Dad into the house and lowered him onto the divan that was closest to the front door. His feet and lower legs hung off the end of it.

Late in the afternoon Alex and I were jumping rope together on the open pavement where our street ended and the field of wild grass defined the end of town. Breathlessly we chanted as we jumped:

Not last night, but the night be-fore
Twenty-four robbers came knocking at my door
I asked them what they wanted,
This is what they said:
Spanish dancer, do some tricks,
Spanish dancer, do some kicks,
Spanish dancer, turn around,
Spanish dancer, touch the ground.
She can do the rhumba,
She can do the splits,
She can wear her dresses
High up to her hips!

Vinny came out of the house and walked determinedly toward the back yard. She usually made fun of us for jumping rope and mocked our rhymes, but she didn't even look at us. She had other things on her mind. There in the back yard, a feathery column of smoke was wafting up from the remains of the garbage fire. Vinny headed toward it.

"Oh no!" Alex screamed when she saw what our sister was carrying. In her open palms Vinny held her own thick golden braids coiled up like a giant snake. The rest of her blond hair hung in uneven shags above her shoulders. I dropped my jump rope. How *could* Vinny have chopped off her long beautiful hair? Why in the world would she do such a thing? Alex and I moved closer to the burn barrel and watched as Vinny tossed one braid into the fire, and then the other. The pungent smell of burning hair filled our nostrils, but we didn't move away.

"Why?" was all Alex could ask, her mouth holding the shape of a little O.

"Braids are for kids," Vinny said.

HALLOWEEN WAS A GRAND and gleeful celebration for the children of Plentywood, whether or not there was already snow on the ground. A dusting, or even a couple of inches, would not stop the eager trick-or-treaters. Vinny and Alex traveled quickly and they were usually able to cover the entire town collecting goodies, always steering clear of the houses where they knew vicious dogs dwelt, especially the one that was home to Killer and Murderer. This year no early snowfall had come to slow the walkers, and I was being allowed to stay out as late as my sisters. When school was over for the day, the three of us rushed home to help our mother make her popcorn balls. Every Halloween she made a giant batch, over a hundred of the gooey treats, to pass out at our door. Buckets of warm popcorn were drizzled with Mother's special sticky sauce, then rolled and packed firmly into balls, and finally wrapped up in wax paper and tied with orange ribbons. Our family's house was an out-of-the-way stop for most treat seekers, but many children walked the extra blocks to collect one of our mother's popcorn balls.

When sundown came and the wind started up its whining, we girls put on our costumes. Each of us had planned her own outfit and now our mother helped with the final touches. Vinny had recently read a thrilling pirate adventure, *Treasure Island,* and she had chosen to dress up like a buccaneer. She wore a pair of Mother's pedal pushers for baggy breeches and a white shirt of Dad's with a wide piece of fabric for a sash. Her black rubber galoshes were good pirate boots and she tucked her pants into them. Mother tied a purple silk scarf around Vinny's short hair, then used her watercolors to paint a thin mustache and a goatee on Vinny's face. Long John Vinny had made herself an eye patch out of black cloth and also a cutlass from two pieces of wood nailed together, and for added realism, she had wrapped tin foil around the blade to make it look like metal.

Alex had completely transformed herself into a gypsy fortuneteller. She wore items of our mother's clothing too—a red silk blouse and a black taffeta skirt, underneath which she piled on several nylon petticoats to make her skirt as voluminous as the Fancy Hat Lady's. Around her neck Alex placed strand after strand of Mother's costume jewelry, many colors of clear glass beads, cultured pearls, and looped chains, and then she encircled her arms with a passel of bracelets. Her long dark hair hung loose below a flowered scarf wound into a turban shape.

Alex used watercolors to paint purple shadows above her eyes, and she added bright red lipstick to her mouth and cheekbones. I was not so elaborately dressed. I just wanted to be a cowboy. I donned my regular denim jeans, although I deeply wished that I was taller so I could borrow Gramp's leather chaps to put over them. I had on a plaid shirt, a little vest, and a red neckerchief under my chin. My own little red cowboy hat looked too much like a cowgirl's so I had borrowed Gramp's brown felt hat from the Pioneer Days celebration. It kept slipping down over my eyes but that just added to my cowboy aw-shucks charm. I hoped that I resembled Jimmy Stewart and Tommy Ryan more than the Pigeon-toed Kid. Vinny loaned me her cap pistol with its leather holster and gun belt, which I tried to wear low-slung across my hips like John Wayne in *The Searchers*, but since I didn't have hips the whole business slid right down to my feet. Mother got a hammer and nail and punched another hole in the belt, and then it stayed snugly and neatly on my waist. I rather lacked the tough-guy swagger I was seeking.

"You don't look very scary," my sisters told me.

"Let's see," said Mother. She dipped her watercolor brush back into the paint and quickly drew a dark, curving moustache and heavy eyebrows on me. "Much better, Black Bart," Mommy said.

We picked up the pillowcases that would hold all our booty and headed out into the night. Vinny carried a flashlight to brighten our way through the areas of town that lacked street lights. As we walked around, the three of us had a jolly time greeting our friends and collecting from the houses all varieties of store-bought candy, as well as homemade fudge, cookies, and cupcakes. A few households gave out oranges or apples, including the town physician, Dr. Sorenson. He answered his door dressed up like a skeleton, and as he handed an apple to each of us, he croaked out, "An apple a day keeps the doctor away, ha-ha-ha-ha!"

We ended our quest for sweets at our grandparents' house.

"Trick or treat!" "Trick or treat!" we called out as we pounded on the kitchen door.

Gramp laughed when he looked into our bags of goodies.

"You girls will be fat as gophers if you eat all of this," he teased.

Grandma Christina topped off our collected treats with the kringle cookies she had baked for the occasion. To me, those Norwegian cookies were perfect for Halloween—they were frightful. I had once watched Grandma prepare a batch of kringle cookies and I was disgusted when I saw that one of the ingredients was mashed-up hard-cooked egg yolks, which she added to the batter along with the sugar and a regular raw egg. When the mixing was complete, the kringles were formed into rings and sprinkled with more sugar before going into the oven. My sisters said that they could not taste the grainy pieces of yolk after the cookies were baked because they were covered with so much sugar, but I knew that I would be able to. The nasty taste of an egg yolk could overpower any sweetness. The kringle cookies were wrapped up in wax paper and secured with a piece of Scotch tape. I carefully placed mine at the bottom of my bag so that stray crumbs could not contaminate the rest of my treats.

"Would you girls like a ride home?" our grandfather offered.

"No thanks, Gramp," we all said. It was much too thrilling to be out on our own on a dark Halloween night with our father's flashlight.

"Then why don't you leave those big bags of loot here? I promise not to eat too much of it, and I can drop off the leftovers tomorrow!" We smiled at Gramp's joking, and we each pulled out a handful of candy to eat on the way home, then we left the heavy pillowcases and Vinny's cutlass in his care.

As the three of us walked through the Old Townsite, Vinny was inspired with a daring idea. "Let's go to the graveyard. Let's see what it's like up there on Halloween, W-O-O-O-O-O-O!" She held the flashlight under her chin to light up her face in a creepy way. She leered like an evil buccaneer.

"All right," said Alex. "But only if you won't do *that* when we get there."

The two of them looked at me. I really did not want to go up the long, unlit road to the dark graveyard, not even with the flashlight along to guide us. I would almost rather eat one of Grandma Christina's hard-boiled egg yolk cookies than go up there at night.

"You can wait down here if you want to," said Vinny. "But I'm taking the flashlight with us." That decided it. Other trick-or-treaters were finishing up their scavenging and they were disappearing from the streets. There were very few street lights in the Old Townsite, and the fingernail moon was not offering much illumination. I certainly did not want to wait there alone in the dark. It would be better to be haunted by ghosts in the company of my sisters.

We passed the new houses at the bottom of the hill, then started up the curving unpaved road. The bare fields on either side were shrouded in darkness but Vinny's light led us on. Once we were well on our way up the slope to the graveyard, a thrill of excitement surged through me. Over the rise of the black hill the crescent moon was hanging by an invisible thread, and the sound of the wind had dropped to a whispering. It seemed that the familiar gravel road, now silvery in the shine of the flashlight, was leading us into a strange and magical new land.

When we reached the flat top of the hill, we paused for a moment as Vinny looked for the packed dirt road that encompassed the cemetery. She found it and then we followed it for a distance. As we passed along, the somber shapes of the tombstones seemed to be aware of our presence; we were trespassers in their place of quiet vigilance. Vinny's flashlight threw a wide circle of brightness onto the ground, and by contrast the spaces of the night beyond the circle seemed blacker than before. Now we were in the the main section of the cemetery but Vinny did not turn back or even slow her pace.

"Are we going to Uncle Rasmus's grave?" I whispered. My feelings of exuberance about this daring undertaking were being overwhelmed by the fearful reality that we were in a pitch black graveyard on Halloween night.

"Yes, now hurry up," Vinny whispered back impatiently. A narrower road made of two dirt tire tracks crossed through the dead grass of the cemetery grounds and over to the section housing our great-uncle's grave on the far edge. Vinny and the beam of the flashlight proceeded onto this passage, and Alex and I scurried to keep up with the moving circle of light. The wind had hushed itself completely, and now the air in the cemetery was cold and perfectly still. Only the soft rustling of Alex's taffeta skirt could be heard on the hill.

Suddenly, across the stillness came the sound of a deep breath, and the three of us froze. It came again. The inhaling noise was like a gasp, then followed a rough exhalation that seemed to go on forever. In sheer terror we stood motionless.

Then, I could not believe what Vinny did. Her infernal curiosity overcame her fear. She slowly raised the beam of the flashlight from the ground and shined it across the grave markers in the direction of the dreadful breathing. Her light finally reached and settled on the form of a hulking figure leaning heavily against one of the tallest monuments in the cemetery. In the dimness we could distinguish no details to tell us whether this creature was a man or a monster, but either possibility was horrific. Vinny turned off the flashlight, took hold of my hand, and began to run along the dirt tire tracks. She was going so fast that my legs flew beneath me. Alex bunched up her skirts and followed as speedily as she could. Gramp's cowboy hat blew off my head as we raced but we could not stop.

The three of us ran to Rasmus Janson's large head tone and crouched behind it, pressing against each other tightly. Our hearts were beating so hard I could hear the beats out loud, a steady thump-thump-thump. No, things were becoming even more terrible. That sound was not our heartbeats. The pounding was coming from the road. The creature was walking toward us.

Again, thump-thump-thump. We knew that sound. It was somewhat muffled by the packed-down dirt of the road, but it could only be the pounding of the big stick carried by the St-St-St-Stick Man. He was coming right toward us. He was probably going to kill us with his stick up there in the dark graveyard where no one would see. Thump-thump-thump. The heavy stick was coming closer.

"Give me the pistol," Vinny whispered.

My fingers fumbled into the holster and pulled out the cap gun. Vinny took it and raised herself slightly to peer around Rasmus's stone. In the pale moonlight she could see that the gigantic form of the St-St-St-Stick Man had left the road and was passing between the graves, and now he was almost upon us. She pointed the cap gun and fired. He stood unmoving and she fired it again. When we used that gun to play Cowboys, the caps sounded loud and almost like real gunshots, but there in the open cemetery they sounded like pathetic little pops, not nearly powerful enough to scare away the St-St-St-Stick Man. Vinny fired the rest of the caps anyway, five more little pops. The metallic smell of the gunpowder lingered over us as we crouched there.

Now the huge man slowly reached out toward the three of us. We shook with fear. Then we saw that he was holding something in his hand.

"Your hat," he said in a low voice. "You lost your hat."

SUNDAY DINNER WAS the most sumptuous meal of the week in Plentywood, and a time for the various generations of a family to sit down together. Grandma Christina and my mother cooked dinner on alternate Sundays, and it was Mother's turn on the first weekend in November. She was preparing my favorite feast—her special fried chicken that was better than anyone else's, mashed potatoes and cream gravy, corn-on-the-cob, carrot and celery sticks, black olives, brown-and-serve rolls, and homemade applesauce. Our grandparents were expected to arrive momentarily, and my older sisters were setting the long dining room table. Mother kept walking into the dining room to look out the picture window. Her dinner was ready and simmering, but Dad had not yet returned from the Courthouse. He rarely worked on the weekend, but he had skipped church service that morning and had gone to his office to do some preparatory work for an upcoming case.

Our grandparents' Oldsmobile drove up and they emerged from it. My sisters and I ran outside to welcome them. Grandma Christina was carrying a rectangular glass pan. She had brought one of her special Jello salads to go with the dinner.

"Christina, you didn't have to bring anything," Mother smiled.

"It's the Waldorf Jello salad from *The Ladies' Home Journal*," Grandma said. "It was supposed to be apple-flavored Jello with the chopped apples, celery, and walnuts, but I substituted lime flavor to make it more colorful. It has a mayonnaise sauce on top"

"Well, it sounds lovely," Lorraine told her mother-in-law, "but you really shouldn't have gone to the trouble."

"Where's Oscar?" asked his parents, and my mother explained about his work. Gramp and Grandma Christina went into the living room to chat with their five grandchildren. The moment Gramp sat down, Katie and Johnny climbed right up into his lap. They poked their small fists into his sides while he tried to maintain a straight face, but soon he was laughing out loud. Almost an hour passed while we waited for my father to return, then Mother telephoned his office. There was no answer.

"He must be on his way," she decided. "Let's sit down and get started." The many dishes of food were brought to the table, and after Grandma said grace, everyone began to eat. Mother conversed cheerfully with Gramp and Grandma but she kept glancing out the big window as she waited for our father to arrive. Christina, too, was watching the street outside.

Mother served an angel food cake for dessert and still Dad had not come home. As I pressed the last soft, tasty crumbs onto my fingertips and dabbed them onto my tongue, I saw my father's car pull into the driveway. A wrinkle spread across Mother's forehead and she pressed her lips tightly together. As Dad walked into the gathering all eyes turned toward him.

"The work took longer than I...."

"You have been drinking, I can smell it," said his mother. Her voice cut like a cold blast of wind into the room. "Drinking on the Sabbath is sinful," she said with a severity that frightened me. She stood up to face him. "Drunk in front of your own children. You should be ashamed, Bud." Her voice quavered with anger. She took a breath and continued, "I know that Vinny had to drive you home from the Veterans. Nellie and Irma told me. And in broad daylight too. What kind of man needs a child to take care of him?" The pitch of her voice rose into shrillness. "A drunk, that's who. A shameful drunk."

Gramp stood up. "Christina, we must go," he said quietly. He wrapped an arm around her shoulders.

Grandma pushed his arm away and leaned forward. Her flat hand swung out and slapped her son hard across his cheek. The loudness of the blow was startling in the silenced room.

Low and bloodlessly came Grandma Christina's next words.

"You have broken my heart."

Ridiculously at such a sad and terrible moment, I thought of the words from *Moonlight Bay*, words that my father had sung to us so many times in the car:

You have stolen my heart,
Now don't go 'way....

But those were not the words I had just heard. Grandma Christina's five words were the worst possible. A stolen heart could be returned, but a broken heart was destroyed.

Gramp's arm circled back around Grandma's shoulders and he gently drew her toward the door. As they passed out of the room I saw the tears glistening on my grandfather's leathery cheeks.

In awful silence the children sat at the dining room table as our parents went into the kitchen. Loud arguing followed until Dad stormed out of the house. Vinny and Alex ran after him and tried to grab his arms to make him stay, but he shook them off. He got into the station wagon and screeched it out of the driveway and drove off.

Many hours later, long after sundown, the family was gathered in the living room when Dad returned. Mother was reading a bedtime story to Katie and Johnny, and we three older girls were stretched out in front of the fireplace reading our library books. It was clear that our father had been drinking more and his red face wore a fearful, ugly scowl. He ignored the quiet scene and went straight to the hall closet. He began throwing things recklessly aside, heaving the coats onto the floor. The wire hangers jangled onto the linoleum. At the back of the closet he found what he was looking for, his hunting rifle.

He pulled it out, and grabbed the box of long bullets on the high shelf in the closet. He carried the gun and bullets into the living room. "What are you doing?" Mother shrieked in alarm.

"You can shut the hell up," our father snarled, pointing the barrel of the gun in her direction. He sat down in his armchair and loaded the rifle, then emptied the rest of the box of bullets into his pocket. Stunned, we all watched him. He got up and took his flashlight from the drawer in the kitchen, then slammed the door hard as he went out into the night.

No one moved for several long minutes, then Mother told Alex to settle Johnny into his crib. "Junior," she said to me, "you take Katie and go to bed too." We did as we were told.

Vinny and Mother went into the basement to get scrap boards, a hammer, and nails from Dad's work table, then Vinny held the boards in place while our mother nailed them across the framing of the outer doors of the living room and kitchen. Folks had never been in the habit of locking their houses in Plentywood, so the custommade doors that Mother had designed did not include locks. Now she made her own.

"Go to bed," she told Alex and Vinny. They went to their bedroom, and Mother paced back and forth in the living room. I could hear her anxious footsteps from where I lay awake in my bed.

Then the sudden sharp peal of a rifle shot split through the silence of the night. Distant but clear. And another sound, its muted whistle as it echoed off the golf course hills. A long silence, and then another shot came, even more distant, and followed by its quiet echo.

As I lay in bed with Katie, she sleeping soundly, I kept listening for the faraway exploding and echoing of the rifle shots, but at last the deepness of the night swallowed them up and the prairie was silent. I must have finally slept, but the next moment it seemed, Mommy had hold of my shoulder and was firmly shaking me awake. It was still dark outside our high bedroom windows. "Jeanne, get up. Pack your clothes in this box. Pack Katie's in here." Mother set two grocery boxes on the foot of our bed.

I sat up and looked stupidly at the boxes. "But, Mommy, they won't all fit," I whimpered as she walked away. Mother spun around.

"Shut up, just shut up. You do as I tell you," she said roughly. My mother had never spoken like that to me before and I sobbed in disbelief.

"Junior, I need you to do this," she said more softly from the doorway. "Whatever you can pack in those boxes. Some school clothes and some play clothes. Do it now."

From the living room windows Vinny could see a diffused rosy light hovering to the east of the golf course hills. She picked up the hammer and used the claw to pry off the boards across the front door and she opened it. Outside, she saw Dad was lying face down on the sidewalk. He had come back home in the middle of the night. When he found the doors would not open, he had beaten on them furiously until his fists were bloodied, then he had passed out right there on the sidewalk. Mother had been sitting up alone in the dark living room, and when the pounding stopped and she saw Dad lying still, she pried open the back door and crept around to the front yard to cover him with blankets and take his car keys.

In the pre-dawn stillness, Vinny and Alex helped Mother load the roof rack and the back of the station wagon while I watched Katie and Johnny. Then Mommy and Alex put the two youngest children in the car and I knew for sure that we were leaving. Vinny, Alex, and I stood for a moment looking at our father where he lay on the hard cement. I felt like all my sense had been drained right from my body. I was completely empty.

"Will Dad be all right?" Alex asked.

"I don't know," said Mother.

The sun rose in a golden glow as the station wagon traveled south. We passed through the familiar countryside and the small towns of Antelope, Medicine Lake, and Froid. Just beyond Culbertson we crossed the splendent Missouri River where it cuts a broad course through abrupt sandstone bluffs. Sunlight sparkled and danced across the wide water, and Gramp's old saw about the swimming rattlesnakes came into my head. They'd be blinded by the spangled waters if they tried to swim across there.

Directly behind Mother, I sat with my cheek pressed hard against the window glass. Unending pools of tears had been flowing from my eyes ever since we left our house, and now my face felt spongy. Alex, too, was weeping on the other side of the seat, while Katie sent peacefully with her head in Alex's lap.

Johnny rested in Vinny's arms on the passenger side up front. Vinny turned around to look at us. Her face was bright with the excitement of the journey, but an expression of pity flickered briefly when she saw that we had been crying.

"It won't be so bad living with Grandpa Parke and Grandma Louise," she said. "There will be lots of things to do there. Bozeman is a real city. We can see the mountains there. Heck, we can climb the mountains there." Vinny had always dreamed of climbing a real mountain, something higher than the chalk buttes.

But I did not feel better when I heard Vinny's words. How could things ever be good again? How would I ever meet as dear a friend as Dale? How would I ever find another teacher as smart and generous as Miss Bergstrom? But mostly, how could I bear not going out to the homestead, and not hearing Gramp's gentle jokes, or watching the corners of his eyes crinkle up with his broad smile?

I had no more tears. I wiped the final dampness from my eyes with the palms of my hands, and again looked out the window.

Along the edge of the highway the speckled patterns of the loose gravel had always caught my attention while traveling in the car. The granular patches of variegated colors were like a continuously changing mosaic as my father's car sped by. Staring at them was mesmerizing as the particles seemed to swirl into circles, and streaks, then back into circles. But now the little rocks were not a visual fascination to me; they were only a relentless reminder of my leaving. The uncountably numerous stones were a measure of the distance, ever increasing, that separated me from the town of my birth, that place I had always known, but would not know so well again.

3 EAST

hf 11.11

rc 10.19 (1